EMOTION: THE POWER OF CHANGE

A Science-based Approach to Ericksonian Hypnosis

DR. G FREDRIC MAU

INCLUDING SCRIPTS FOR:
HYPNOTIC INDUCTION
RAPID INDUCTION
HYPNOTIC DEPTH TESTING
PAIN ALLEVIATION
FEARS
REGRESSIONS

WatermarkColumbia.com
Facebook.com/WatermarkHypnosis
Twitter.com/WatermarkCola

DEDICATION

To my wife, Sandy, who has supported me along the twisting and strange path of learning hypnosis, becoming a therapist, building a practice, and now writing a book.

Why You Should Buy This Book Now, or You Have to Know Why Things Work on a Starship

In the middle of a battle with Khan (Ricardo Montalbán, not Benedict Cumberbatch), Captain Kirk and Mr. Spock start fooling around with the command console on the Enterprise. Lt. Saavik does not understand why, and Kirk replies, "You have to learn *why* things work on a starship." Kirk has a cool plan to outperform Khan because he knows more about how things work than Khan does (Meyer, 1982).

In 1995 the National Institutes of Health issued a report strongly recommending hypnosis to treat chronic pain and insomnia. The report noted that the mechanism for the relief of pain and insomnia was not well understood.

Much has changed since 1995. Advances in neurology and neuroimaging brain scans now reveal exactly how suggestive processes and hypnosis function. The brain physiology of hypnosis is well understood.

In 1784, French king Louis XVI appointed a royal commission headed by Benjamin Franklin to investigate amazing cures by the flamboyant Franz Anton Mesmer, a man with plenty of style and a frightening, misunderstood power. The commission found that there was no science to what Mesmer was doing, only suggestion. If only Franklin's commission had access to functional magnetic imagery brain scans—they could have seen how the power of suggestion changes not just the mind, but also the brain.

The reality is that emotion changes behavior. Stories frame and create our emotions. These changes are not just "mental" or ephemeral; they cause profound physical changes in the brain and profound metaphysical changes in the very meaning of our lives.

This book is extensively documented with peer-reviewed empirical studies (just flip back to the References on page 92 and check it out). It provides you with instruction not only on how to perform hypnosis, but on how hypnosis works: This is the scientific data, the "why" that you need to know.

Most of our models of change are cognitive. They are about learning new information, and then trying (and often failing) to implement it. Emotional change is different from cognitive approaches, and powerful.

You want to be a great hypnotist. You want to know more than just how to perform tricks. You need to know why things work on a Starship. Buy this book, read, learn, enjoy.

Contents

1 WHAT IS HYPNOSIS?

The word "hypnotism," coined by Scottish Surgeon Dr. James Braid in 1842, covers a number of phenomena. The word comes from the Greek term for "sleep," although hypnosis does not involve physical sleep. At the most basic level hypnosis is the art of suggestion. Training in hypnosis involves learning to use language in emotionally suggestive ways as a catalyst for profound personal change.

Levels of Relaxation

One way to look at classic clinical hypnosis is as a relaxation phenomenon. When you are completely awake, alert, and conscious, your brain wave cycles can be up to 20 cycles per second (hertz, or Hz). This is the electric cycle of the brain as measured by an electroencephalograph (EEG) machine. Wide-awake consciousness occurs in a range from 14 to 20 Hz and is called Beta level awareness.

Most of us have had the experience of doing something we really enjoy and losing track of time. We've also had the experience of being stuck trying to solve a problem, make a decision, or do something creative—only to have a Eureka! moment the next morning in the shower. As John Steinbeck said, "It is a common experience that a problem difficult at night is resolved in the morning after the committee of sleep has worked on it" (1954, p. 107). This relaxed, creative state is Alpha level relaxation, at a cycle of 9 to 14 Hz. The hallmarks of Alpha state are creativity and losing track of time. Think about it: Creativity is not a rational process. Creativity occurs when an unconscious part of you sees connections and solutions which you did not see before and you have an "a-ha" experience.

On the other end of the spectrum, true sleep, where you can dream, occurs at 4 Hz or less (down to about 1.5 Hz), and is termed deep Delta sleep.

Between Alpha and Delta is Theta level relaxation, 4 to 9 Hz. Most of us have had the experience of dozing off while watching TV or reading late at night. Anyone seeing you would think you were asleep, but you know you are really not asleep. Think of a husband snoring on the sofa while "watching" a ball game. Theta is the dreamy state of falling asleep (or the luxurious time waking up on a non-rushed morning). In this state, cortisol, the body's primary stress hormone, decreases. Feel-good happy neurotransmitters like beta-endorphins and serotonin increase, providing a wonderful experience. Theta also involves being more emotionally open. Classic clinical hypnosis involves relaxation to this level.

It is important to note that hypnotic language can be used to promote emotional change at any of the levels of consciousness. The great hypnotist and physician Milton Erickson describes hypnotic work in the "ordinary waking state" many times in his writings (cf. Erickson & Rossi, 1975). It is also interesting to note that the word "trance" is used to describe both a relaxed Theta state and an ecstatic and energized upper Beta state (both of which provide experiences outside the normal range of emotional familiarity, and thus create greater suggestibility).

Deep Relaxation

The voice in your head that you think of as *you* is called your executive function. The executive function is a function of the prefrontal areas of the frontal lobe (a portion of the brain located just behind the forehead). During sleep, the frontal lobe naturally goes offline. The best way to visualize this may be to think of a light bulb on a dimmer switch slowly dimming down.

Classic relaxed hypnotic suggestibility is associated with frontal inhibition (Gruzelier, Gray, & Horn, 2002; Jamieson, & Sheehan, 2004; Gruzelier, 2006). There is also deactivation of the executive function in the frontal lobe during hypnotic relaxation (Schjoedt, Stødkilde-Jørgensen, Geertz, Lund, & Roepstorff, 2009).

While the frontal lobe naturally relaxes into sleep, other parts of your brain continue to be engaged, of course. This relaxation of the rational or cognitive process of the brain allows hypnotic work to be done at a more emotional level, by engaging more emotional parts of the brain. Since emotions—not information—drive behavior, this relaxation creates a process of change which is more rapid and operates on a deeper level than cognitive changes.

Of course, the more emotional or non-rational parts of you are still you. You are always active in framing and creating changes. Hypnosis is a process for greater self-control. Even a skilled hypnotherapist cannot take you anywhere you do not want to go, but he or she can help you create profound changes that seem out of reach at a conscious level.

What about Stage or Entertainment Hypnosis?
Stage work is different from clinical hypnosis, but can involve the same relaxation phenomena. Other processes are also involved in stage work, such as creating compliance, using trivial commitments or "yes sets" to move people into a hypnotic state, and even performance pressure from the audience. Stage hypnotists are also typically interested in finding participants who are very directly suggestible (they relax into hypnosis easily with direct suggestions) and highly physically suggestible (they actually do what is suggested while in the hypnotic state, rather than simply engaging in it as a mental process). None of these factors are significant for clinical hypnosis.

It is important to remember that all hypnotic phenomena rely on a relationship of mutual rapport and trust between the hypnotist and the participant. When someone goes up on a stage, she or he is giving the hypnotist a tremendous amount of psychological permission—that is, the person knows the nature of the show and wants to participate. If your reaction to a stage show is that it is not for you, it is unlikely that you would make a good participant.

In a clinical setting, rapport between the hypnotherapist and the client is critical. Stephens, Silbert, & Hasson (2010) found brain activity aligning between individuals during effective communication—that is, the brain wave patterns of two people having a "great conversation"—tend to become the same.

2 EMOTION IS THE POWER OF CHANGE

Emotion and Change

Emotion, not information, drives behavior and frames belief. Emotion provides the power for change to occur. Think about the power and speed of emotional change. Neurologically, it takes one-fifth of a second to fall in love (Ortigue, et al., 2010, cf. "Syracuse," 2010). Religious conversion is another example of rapid emotional shift that results in dramatic life changes. Both falling in love and religious conversion usually follow a process, but the moment of profound change is powerful and virtually instantaneous. Hypnosis is a tool for facilitating that sort of change.

Motivational Interviewing (Miller & Rollnick, 2002) is a counseling process which is very much like Erickson's waking state hypnosis. The process is helpful in a variety of counseling situations, but was developed to address substance abuse. For example, Hester and Miller (2003, p. 19) found motivational enhancement to be the second most effective means of addressing alcohol dependence—far more effective than 12-Step programs, confrontational interventions, or education. Regarding this approach, Miller asks:

> How is it that having a single session of motivational interviewing before beginning a course of outpatient or inpatient rehabilitation program can double a person's chances of abstinence three months later? The person has learned no new coping skills or conditioned responses, and there have been no changes in the "actual" external contingencies operating in

the person's life. ("Competing Motivations," Miller, 1998, para. 5)

His answer is, "Whatever it is, it seems to involve a sudden shift in meaning... In another sense, it is as if the person steps outside the self for a moment, to see himself or herself from another perspective" ("Competing Motivations," Miller, 1998, para. 4). *It is the change of emotional meaning which is critical for life change.*

It is important to realize that these changes are real. In a pivotal scene in J. K. Rowling's novel, *Harry Potter and the Deathly Hallows*, Harry asks Dumbledore, "Tell me one last thing: is this real, or has this been happening inside my head?" Dumbledore replies, "Of course it is happening inside your head, Harry, but why on earth should that mean it is not real?" (2007, p. 723). The great golfer Bobby Jones is famously quoted as saying, "Competitive golf is played mainly on a five-and-a-half-inch course, the space between your ears." In this case what is true of golf is true of life.

Psychiatry makes the argument, *change the brain, change the mind*. In other words, all mental functions are the result of brain function (Kandel, 1998). I believe the door swings the other way; studies show that *change the mind, change the brain* works as well (Ray, 2004).

In a 2008 study Plassman, et al., presented people with two wines in a taste test. The first was a $5 cabernet sauvignon, presented as it was—a $5 wine—but also labeled as a $45 wine. The second was a $90 cabernet sauvignon, presented as it was—a $90 wine—but also labeled as a $10 wine. Subjects were asked which wine tasted better, and predictably, the wine labeled as more expensive was judged to be better. More importantly, functional magnetic resonance imaging (fMRI) brain scans utilized during the study found substantial changes in the pleasure centers of the brain associated with the wine presented as more expensive. Regardless of the actual quality of the wine tasted, the belief and emotional framing associated with a particular wine created the reality of the experience—the more "expensive" wine was judged to be better—even though the wines were the same. *This change happened at the level of brain physiology.*

You Are the Story You Tell Yourself

"I don't even know why I'm here," my client began as he flopped down into the chair. "I got laid off this week. I feel so miserable I didn't even want to get out of bed this morning."

A couple of days later an unrelated client came in: "I've gotta tell you, doc. I got laid off from my job this week. I always hated that job, but I don't know if I'd ever have had the courage to quit. I'm polishing up my resume—this is a new beginning for me!"

Clearly the same thing is *not* the same thing. The Greek philosopher Epictetus is quoted as saying, "People are disturbed not by things, but by the view which they take of them." Being laid off has real-world consequences, since most people want to be able to eat and keep a roof over their heads. But for one man the same news was the end of the world, and for the other it was a new start. Their emotional realities could not be more different.

The Narrative Therapist G. S Howard wrote:

People tell themselves stories that infuse certain parts of their lives and actions with great meaning and de-emphasize other aspects. But had any of them chosen to tell himself or herself a somewhat different story, the resulting pattern of more-meaningful and less-meaningful aspects of his or her life would have been quite different. (1989, p. 168)

Ericksonian hypnosis is about using stories and narratives to channel and frame emotion. The process of change is not based on rational arguments, cognitive processing, or insights into the past. It is about creating a new emotional meaning, about seeing the world in a profoundly new way. The goal of a hypnotic process is to help the client create that sort of change of perspective.

Ericksonian Hypnosis

Many traditional approaches to change focus on finding insight— that is, discovering the cause of the emotional problem. Many others focus on cognitive or rational change. Erickson's approach to change is fundamentally different:

> Insight is not necessary for change. As a matter of fact, hypnosis or indirection is frequently used to bypass conscious processes—and therefore to work utilizing unconscious processes. The unconscious is regarded as a vast storehouse of learning and as a context—in itself—for change. Such a view is a revolutionarily different conception of the nature and scope of the unconscious. In contrast to the traditional psychodynamic notion of the unconscious as a place full of negative forces, impulses, and ideas which are so unacceptable that they must be repressed from conscious awareness, Erickson had a positive view of the unconscious. (Feldman, 1985, p. 155)

The goal in Ericksonian hypnosis is to help the client create a new emotional story or narrative, so that he or she sees things in a profoundly different way. This is the catalyst for emotional change. The client brings her or his story, his or her emotional reality to the session. As she or he explores and embraces new stories, that emotional reality changes.

3 PACING, LEADING, & SUCCESS

Classic clinical hypnosis involves helping a client unwind into a relaxed state on the borderline of sleep—Theta level relaxation. This has been referred to as a trance state. This level of relaxation is helpful for addressing problems at a more emotional level, rather than cognitively. However, hypnosis is fundamentally the art of suggestion, and hypnotic or emotionally suggestive language can be used at any of the levels of consciousness, including the ordinary waking state. The best research indicates that a trance state is not real (Kirsch & Lynn, 1995; Lilenfeld & Arkowitz, 2009), and that emotional buy-in by clients and skillful suggestion by hypnotists is the key to hypnotic change. Fundamentally, hypnosis is based on a relationship of mutual rapport and trust between a client and a hypnotist.

Pacing and Leading
"Oh my god, what an awful day!" my client blurted, loudly, as she walked, sopping wet, into my waiting room. "It's pouring rain, my manager dumped crap on me all day, and on the way over here, I kept getting cut off on the Interstate! Then I found out that I've lost my umbrella, and it's pouring rain here!"

At that moment I knew I couldn't work with her—that is, in her current emotional state we would not be able to do anything emotionally significant. As the professional hypnotist, it was my job to reframe things for her.

"I know exactly what you mean!" I said, a little loudly. "I got cut off on the freeway this morning coming in. It's been that sort of day all over." And then, softening my tone a bit as I went along: "But isn't it nice to know you can come i

9

somewhere like this, take a deep breath, and do something different with your day?"

In hypnosis, the process of emotionally joining with a client is known as *pacing*. Once this emotional link is developed, the goal of the hypnotist is to lead the client to positive change (Feldman, 1985). Pacing involves stepping into the client's emotional reality, and walking with her or him to create a genuine emotional connection. By matching her emotional tone, I was able to establish myself as my client's ally; this is pacing. If I had said something like, "Oh hey, it's not that bad," I would have become her emotional adversary. By emotionally joining with her, I established rapport. Stephens, Silbert, and Hasson (2010) found the brain states of individuals mirror each other during effective communication. Popular press reports of this refer to it as "mind melds" (cf. Coghlan, 2010; Vergano, 2010).

The rapport established by pacing is deeper than verbal exchange; this emotional link is created at a deep neurological level. It is based on the body's mirror neuron system. This is the system that picks up on the emotional context exhibited by people around you (Blakeslee, 2006).

Mirror neurons are the basis of a mechanism that creates a direct link between the sender of a message and its receiver. Thanks to this mechanism, actions done by other individuals become messages that are understood by an observer, without even thinking about it. (Rizzolatti & Craighero, 2004, p. 183)

Pacing with a client creates the context for leading her or him to positive change. Once I had established pacing ("I know exactly what you mean!"), I was able to lead her to a better place ("Isn't it nice to know you can...do something different with your day?").

Pacing begins as soon as the client has contact with you. It can involve the emotional message you send via your website or ads. It certainly involves the physical setup and decor of your waiting room and office. Your decor should be based on the emotional states you wish to create for your clients as they come in the door. My intentional goals are to create a space which is attractive, friendly, professional, comfortable, and credible. All the art and decor is directed toward those goals. Intentionality and pacing should apply to your personal, nonverbal communication. Most people make a very broad "yes" or "no" decision within four seconds of meeting someone, based on physical appearance—including facial expressions, body language, and attire (Hogan, 2005, pp. 17-18).

Pacing certainly begins as soon as you speak with the client. Remember to be present in the moment and attuned to what the client is saying. Via your mirror neuron system, you will pick up on his or her nonverbal cues. Pay attention to how you feel. Remember that hypnotic or suggestive language can be used in any state of consciousness, so begin to use suggestion to positively frame the encounter from the start. Look for ways to begin to lead; that is, to begin to focus the client on her or his successful outcome.

Focus on Success

The initial part of a clinical hypnosis session is usually a pre-talk, or coaching time. The goal is to find out what has happened with the client since the last session, to focus on success or successful exceptions (even if success is not complete), and to listen for the client's emotional language. Although you must be engaged and present with the client, it is a good idea to jot brief notes of the actual words the client uses to describe solutions or problems. Try not to suggest terms to clients; your goal is to discover how he or she frames these things in her or his own language. While it is not usually best to parrot these phrases back to the client in normal waking conversation, you will want to use (and sometimes bend) these phrases during the relaxed state.

Particularly in the first session, you may want to use de Shazer's Miracle Question:

Suppose [pause] after we finish here, you go home tonight, watch TV, do your usual chores, et cetera, and then go to bed and to sleep [pause] and, while you are sleeping, a miracle happens [pause] and, the problem that brought you here is solved, just like that! [pause]. But, this happens while you are sleeping, so you cannot know that it has happened [pause]. Once you wake up in the morning, how will you go about discovering that this miracle has happened to you?" (1997, pp. 375-376).

This is an excellent question to prompt the client to give success language back to you. Another great question to begin a first session is, "Once you make this change, how will your life be better?" The question, of course, suggests that change will happen, and life will be better. You might want to begin subsequent sessions by asking, "How have things improved this week?" or "What sort of success have you seen this week?" Even if the success is scant, focus on it as success, and state that the purpose of the process is to create more success.

4 INDUCTIONS

Once you have established pacing and leading, you are ready to move into more traditionally conceived relaxation hypnosis. The induction is the process of helping someone relax. From this point on I will provide some scripts, but with a note of caution: Scripts are just guidelines. It is important to translate them into your own language; that is, into language which feels natural for you. It is also important to incorporate your client's specific goals and emotional language into the session. A beginning hypnotist can use scripts to become comfortable with patterns of hypnotic language. However, as you mature as a hypnotist, you should become less dependent upon scripts.

Script: A Basic Introduction
This is not really a relaxation script – it is for the waking state. Remember, you are constantly framing the emotional environment for your client's success. This is some patter I use to begin the first hypnosis session, after the pre-talk or coaching.

In my office, my clients sit in a recliner that has a lever used to rock back. I record the client processes on CDs, and I use a light and sound machine, set to a Theta setting, as a distraction or relaxation device (do not use this device if your client has a history of epilepsy or seizures; I screen clients for this on my intake form, and if they check "yes," I just leave out all mention of the device). You will want to adjust your delivery based on your actual equipment.

Throughout this book, the language of scripts is in *italic* print.

Okay, the next thing I'm going to do is take about a minute to explain the mechanics of the process we're going to do today, then we are going straight into the hypnosis process. Before we do that, is there anything else you would like to ask me or tell me?

Okay, in just a moment I'm going to invite you to lean back. There is a lever on the right-hand side of the chair. You'll probably find that you need to scoot back a bit in the chair as you lean back, but it is very comfortable. I always have a blanket for you to cover up with if you would like that.

Today we're going to use a relaxation device, which looks a lot like this [hold up the light and sound machine glasses]. *You know how it feels when you walk into a room where music is playing and you just want to move with the music? This works the same way—you'll have your eyes comfortably closed. You'll see a little flash of light through your eyelids. It doesn't have to be particularly bright or dim, just comfortable. I will adjust it until it is comfortable for you. The light has a rhythm and a cycle to it; as the light cycles down, just go with it. Remember we're trying to get to a brain state of 5 or 6 cycles per second. You'll also be wearing some headphones. In the headphones you will hear some music, some beeping* [this is from the light and sound machine], *and my voice. You want my voice to be in the foreground as the main thing you hear, with the music and beeping in the background. I'll adjust all those levels until they are comfortable for you.*

At that point all you need to do is relax. You don't need to try to relax, you don't have to help me in any way. Just let your mind go. This is your time to daydream.

Seriously, we're probably the only learning method in the world where we will tell you, "Please don't pay attention to what I am saying." You can think about the beach or the mountains or the dog—even if you don't have a dog— whatever is relaxing for you. Just drift and daydream.

I am going to record this and give you the only recording, so don't worry about missing anything. You will have that— and you won't be talking anyway while you are under.

Different people have different subjective experiences with hypnosis. Some people feel like they hear everything I'm saying, others feel like they zone out and miss the whole thing. Still others feel like they're hearing everything, but then, whoa! they feel like they're coming back from somewhere. Whatever you feel, it is appropriate for you. Your subconscious mind knows what is best for you, and that's what's going to happen now.

Hypnosis is a learned skill: The more you do it, the deeper you go! You're going to have a great experience today, and as we do more it will get better and better.

Okay, here are the glasses...

This is really the waking component of the induction. It is designed to frame the client's experience of hypnosis in a positive way.

One additional note: As my clients lean back in the chair and get comfortable, I make it a point to attend briefly to my recording equipment or clinical notes. It will not help your rapport with your client if she (or he) thinks you are checking her out. Always maintain complete professionalism with a client, and keep in mind the code of ethics of our profession.

Script: A Progressive Relaxation Induction with Ego Strengtheners

Every hypnotist should know a basic progressive relaxation process. I've incorporated some positive affirmations into this one. By this time the client is wearing the light and sound glasses, and has on headphones, with music playing. If you are not using any technology, you can just ask him or her to close the eyes, breathe deeply, and relax.

Just close your eyes, and allow your thoughts to drift. Just breathing in deeply, and breathing out completely. Breathing in deeply, and breathing out completely. Allowing your breathing to become very deep and rhythmic, very natural and spontaneous.

And already beginning to notice the gentle feelings of relaxation moving through your body, which is good for deep hypnosis. Now I don't know whether your feet feel so heavy it is as though they are melting. Or perhaps your hands feel very light, or very heavy, or there may be the gentle pulse of relaxation in the tips of your fingers, as your heart beats rhythmically, naturally, normally. Or perhaps your eyelids are so so very heavy that they simply will not open. Whatever you feel, it is appropriate for you. Your powerful subconscious mind knows just what is best for you, now.

I'd like to invite you to notice your feet, your feet which feel so so heavy, the toes melting into the arch of the foot, melting into the heel, so relaxed and so comfortable now. You can feel the relaxation flowing across the ankle. You are learning to have faith, and let go. You are learning to get rid of 'shoulds' and 'musts.'

As the relaxation flows from the ankle to the knees, notice that the muscles of the shins and calves are melting and flowing, so comfortable. You are learning to trust yourself and your own instincts. You are listening to that calm, still, always peaceful voice inside.

And you can feel the relaxation beginning to flow across the knees toward the hips, as the large muscles of the thighs simply dissolve, melting away, so comfortable. You are learning that fear and excitement are two sides of the same coin. You are realizing that you are not defined by how much you make or how you earn it.

I wonder if you would like to increase the relaxation in your neck and shoulders now, or if you would rather try to keep that stress a little longer while other parts of the body relax first. You happiness does not depend upon others.

As you can feel the relaxation flowing now, across the hips, into the abdomen. Your breathing is so deep. With each breath in, the muscles of the diaphragm contract, and as those muscles release now, you naturally breathe out, letting go, relaxing. Allowing the inner organs of the abdomen to move in their rhythmic, natural functions, and feeling the relaxation beginning to move, vertebra by vertebra up the back, as the muscles of the back melt away. You are beginning to discover and like yourself. You are experiencing life in a new way, through different eyes, from better and healthier perspectives.

Over 21 thousand times a day you breathe in deeply, and breathe out completely. Over 86 thousand times a day your heart beats rhythmically, naturally, normally, circulating oxygen and nutrients and fresh new ideas from the tips of your toes to the tip of your nose, so feel the relaxation flowing from the shoulders to the elbows, from the elbows to the wrists, from the wrists to the tips of the fingers, where you might feel that gentle pulse of relaxation. You are finding ways to appreciate 'old' things in 'new' ways.

Imagine the muscles of the neck and shoulders like heavy ropes coming untied, and just flopping on the floor. Imagine the muscles of the jaw relaxing and melting, perhaps allowing the lips to part slightly, as you continue to breathe in deeply and breathe out completely. You are literally becoming a new person as the days go by. You can release, set free, let go of situations, people, events and thoughts.

Some people actually hold stress, strain even confusion in the tiny muscles of the eyes and forehead. Imagine the hands and feet actually opening up and all stress, all strain, all confusion, all negative emotion such as anger, shame, guilt, and resentment flowing out of the body. These emotions no longer serve you and you will no longer serve them. They will be removed from your mind, gone from your thoughts, gone even from your body's awareness, so free and flexible you simply let them go. So feel the deep relaxation. Everything is not under your control, and that's a very good thing.

—As the eyes are so heavy, so heavy that they simply will not open. They are just glued shut. In fact, you try to open your eyes and find you cannot and you go deeper. You try and you cannot and you go deeper now. You are learning to flow with the current and absorb its positive energy throughout your body. So feel the muscles of the scalp melt away. So relaxed, so comfortable. Completely at peace. You open yourself up to see the world for what it truly is; you see with clarity and you do not judge what you clearly see, you accept. Within you is your healing power; it is safe to be you—you can safely and calmly step into your future.

Script: Beauty, a Guided Imagery

You can do guided imagery of any scene. People often enjoy the beach, or a mountain glade. You can even ask your client, during the pre-talk, "If you could be anywhere, your most relaxing place, where would that be?" and then base your guided imagery on the response. This induction leaves the place open, and invites the client to create his or her own reality. The more vague the suggestions are, the more the client is invited to fill in the vibrancy and details of it from her or his own mind.

Just relax and breathe deeply, letting your breathing become deep and rhythmic, natural and spontaneous, and already noticing the gentle sensations of relaxation moving through your body, which is good for deep hypnosis.

And as you continue to relax deeply now, noticing just how good you feel, I begin to wonder just how good you can feel. I wonder what if you can imagine what it would feel like if you were seven or ten times more relaxed and comfortable.

And of course you know that if you think of a beautiful place, you can relax more deeply, so I'd like to invite you, if you like, to imagine the most beautiful place you can think of. This could be some place you've been, or someplace you'd like to go, or just a fantasy of a place—so relaxed and so comfortable that it is easy to allow the body to relax now, everything to relax now.

As you think of this beautiful place, or just pretend or imagine it, because that's fine too, as you continue to relax and go deeper now, step into it. Feel it. Be there in that moment, breathe it in. Notice how comfortable it feels, the temperature. Hear anything that is being said, if anything is said, or any other sounds, or fragrances.

Notice how easily, how comfortably your body moves in this place, and just enjoy this moment as you continue to wonder just how good you can feel, now...

Script: A Confusion Induction

Progressive relaxation or guided imagery inductions may not work best for highly analytical people. The intent of a confusion induction is to make it seem to make sense, but wrap in and out in such a way that the words are impossible to follow. The goal is to cause the client to just give up and drift off. This is my reworking of an anonymous script.

Just close your eyelids and let your mind drift where it will.

You are aware of everything, and yet you are not aware. You are listening with your subconscious mind, while your conscious mind is far away, and not listening. Your conscious mind is far away, and not listening. Your subconscious mind is listening, and listening, and hearing everything while your conscious mind remains very relaxed and peaceful. You can relax peacefully because your subconscious mind is taking charge, and when this happens, you close your eyes and let your subconscious do all the listening. Your subconscious mind knows, and because your subconscious mind knows, your conscious mind does not need to know and can stay deeply asleep, and not mind while your subconscious mind listens.

You have much potential in your subconscious mind which you don't have in your conscious mind. You can remember everything that has happened with your subconscious mind, but you cannot remember everything with your conscious mind. You can forget so easily, and with forgetting certain things you can remember other things. Remembering what you need to remember, and forgetting what you can forget. It does not matter if you forget, you need not remember what you can forget. Your subconscious mind remembers everything that you need to know and you can let your subconscious mind listen and remember while your conscious mind sleeps and forgets. With your eyes closed, comfortable, listen with your subconscious mind, and when you're listening very, very carefully, your conscious mind will not mind what it forgets because your subconscious mind is taking care of you.

As you continue to listen to me, with your subconscious mind, your conscious mind sleeps deeper and deeper, and deeper, and deeper. Let your conscious mind stay deeply asleep, and let your subconscious mind listen to me.

You can relax peacefully because your subconscious mind is taking charge, and when this happens, you close your eyes and let your subconscious do all the listening. Your subconscious mind knows, and because your subconscious mind knows, your conscious mind does not need to know and can stay deeply asleep, and not mind while your subconscious mind listens. You can let your subconscious mind listen and remember while your conscious mind sleeps and forgets. With your eyes closed, comfortable, listen with your subconscious mind, and when you're listening very, very carefully, your conscious mind will not mind what it forgets because your subconscious mind is taking care of you.

As you continue to listen to me, with your subconscious mind, your conscious mind sleeps deeper and deeper, and deeper, and deeper. Let your conscious mind stay deeply asleep, and let your body relax so comfortably now.

Another great confusion induction is in Havens and Walters (1989, pp. 54-56), "Confusion induction script."

Script: The Three Lessons—A Guided Imagery with Confusion Elements

This induction is not original with me. I've known it for years, but have no idea where it came from. I can't find it on the Internet, or in any of the books I have. It is one of my favorites, so here goes. If it is yours, please let me know!

I'm going to count down now from ten to one, and as I count backward I'm going to tell you a little story called The Three Lessons. As those numbers go down, I'd like to invite you to imagine yourself relaxing even deeper and deeper into an ever more comfortable state of relaxation.

Ten...nine...Once, not too long ago, there was a young girl who lived in another state. I don't remember if it was in Washington or Texas or someplace else. Eight...seven...She heard about a wise older woman who lived deep in the woods, and she figured that the wise woman was someone who could help her with her problem, so she searched and found directions to her house, and once she did, she set out through the forest.

Six...five...It was late October, and it was cold. She could see her breath, and as she passed an icy stream, she bent down and put her hand into the cold, cold water. Eventually, up ahead in a clearing she saw the house...

And when she got there she knocked on the door. From inside she heard a voice which said, "You may come in," which was lesson number one. Four...three...It was warm in the house, and she looked around at all the things in there...

Finally, she could resist no longer and blurted out, "I want to know everything you know so I can help myself with my problem!"

The wise woman looked deeply into the girl's eyes and said, "You already know everything that you need to know, except that you don't yet know that you already know all those things," which was lesson number two.

Finally, as it was nearing the time for the time for her to go, the young girl didn't know if a minute had passed or an hour. She looked up again at the wise woman who said, "You must listen very closely," which was lesson number three. The young woman left, and we know everything worked out just fine for her, two...and one....

Non-Clinical Inductions
It is always fun to have some gee-whiz inductions up your sleeve. You probably won't use these in a clinical setting with clients, but they are fun to break out at a party when someone asks what you do, and you tell them you're a hypnotist. You'll probably be asked to do some hypnosis— so have some fun!

Remember, though, that hypnosis can engage serious emotions, so be ready to frame things positively for your participant, and help him or her to be all right as you wrap things up.

Script: Swinging Watch Induction
You can use this with a swinging watch, pendant, crystal, or necklace. If you borrow a necklace, be sure she tells you who to hand it to while she is under.

Also, you really won't do this one with a script (that wouldn't be cool when you're showing off at a party, anyway), since you're having to manage the watch and keep

21

an eye on the subject. Just get the gist down, and use the suggestive language.

Swing the watch (or whatever item) two to four inches in front of the subject's eyes, with it swinging so that the outer arc is about the width of the subject's face. This induction actually involves a little cheat; the tiny muscles of the eyes are not designed to follow such a motion at close range, so they will become fatigued very quickly. When you say, "You're getting sleepy, your eyelids are getting heavy," the subject's eyes will be feeling a bit tired. Also notice that in hypnosis, "try" is the language of failure—suggest that the subject "try" something you don't want to happen.

Okay, just focus your eyes on the watch, watching the watch as it swings back and forth, back and forth, back and forth.

Now, I'm not going to tell you to close your eyes now, but you already can feel your eyes. Your eyes which are already becoming so heavy, so very heavy. Focusing all your attention on the watch, watching it swing, swing, swing, back and forth, back and forth, back and forth.

You can try to keep your eyes open, noticing it is harder and harder to try to keep your eyes open, harder and harder.

And I'm not going to tell you to close your eyes now [notice that this is actually a veiled direct command to do just that], *but there is a part of you which already knows just how good it will feel to close your eyes now, a part of you which knows just how relaxed you will feel as you close your eyes now...*

Your eyelids which are getting so very heavy now, and you know now how comfortable it will be when you close your eyes now, just imagining how comfortable you would like to be as you close your eyes now, so you can relax so deeply as you close your eyes now,

And SLEEP, SLEEP, SLEEP, deeper now, more relaxed than ever before, each breath takes you deeper, each word takes you deeper, more comfortable, more relaxed, completely at peace...

Watching the subject's eyes, you may need to keep up the "your eyes are so heavy" patter for a bit. Note that if a subject still has his or her eyes open after two or three minutes of this, it indicates significant resistance—she or he has to be working very hard at that point in order to keep the eyes open. Just point that out, and suggest that another time and place, and type of hypnosis might be better for him or her.

NOTE: Do NOT tell your subject that he or she "can't be hypnotized." For one thing, it is not true. Every person relaxes to Theta many times a day; it is a natural process. Additionally, everyone takes emotional suggestions. Manage the situation so that you don't fail and your subject does not fail. Simply suggest that this may not be the best setting or hypnosis approach for her or him, and thank your subject for being a good sport.

Script: Candle Flame

This is a mindfulness or focus induction. It can be done with any object, so you might do this induction while asking the subject to focus into the palm of his or her hand, or to concentrate all her or his focus on a spot on the wall or the corner of the ceiling. You might even use this in a clinical setting with a client. I like to use a candle flame if I'm at a party where there are candles, because the flickering flame gives the whole thing a nice quality. The candle is on the coffee table just in front of your subject's seat (not close to her or his face or in his or her hand). Again, there is a tiny cheat here—it is hard to keep your eyes open without blinking, so a bit of fatigue may set in.

Okay, just sit back and relax, allowing your body to be heavy and comfortable in that chair, and just focusing your attention on the candle flame, trying to keep your eyes on the flame, staring into the flame, and noticing how it flickers, how bright and white it is.

And at the same time noticing just how comfortable your body is. Staring at the flame, flickering. And how deep and comfortable your breathing is, as you continue to focus all your attention on the flickering flame, noticing how it moves, how bright it is. And your breathing, so deep, outside sounds and influences just take you deeper, and as you continue to focus all your attention into the flame, notice that you are looking into the very heart of it, the brightness of it, watching it flicker, noticing that your eyes are becoming so heavy, as you continue to focus all your attention into that tiny, beautiful, dancing flame.

And of course part of you knows just how good it will feel when you allow your eyes to close now, when your eyes close now, just continuing to imagine that flame, flickering, and carrying all your attention into the flame, breathing deeply now, your body heavy and comfortable now, and eyes closed now

And sleep, sleep, sleep, deeper now...

Emerging

Since hypnosis does not actually involve Delta level sleep, it is not really appropriate to talk in terms of "awakening" a client or subject. The standard term for bringing someone out of hypnosis is "emerging." The emerging can be very simple:

You are now coming back into the room, back into the room. Wide awake! Eyes wide open! And you feel good!

Sometimes hypnotists count people up from hypnosis. By convention counting down is used for inductions and counting up is used for emerging, but it really does not matter which way you count.

When I count from one to five you will be completely awake, totally alert, feeling very good. One, becoming more and more aware of the room around you. When you are ready Two feel good for no reason at all, then Three your eyes will open and you will be Four wide awake! Wide awake feeling refreshed and renewed. And Five – Eyes wide open, wide awake! And you feel good!

If you are recording the process, you might want to do a double emerging. This is actually a deepener (a further induction embedded within a process), which invites the person to relax even more deeply into Delta sleep, combined with an emerging.

Deepener: *As you are listening to my voice, so relaxed now, if this is a time a place and a space for you to sleep, then you can let yourself drift into a deep, refreshing sleep. At the right moment you can simply turn off the player, if you like, and as your head touches the pillow this is your opportunity to allow your mind to drift, your thoughts to flow. Let yourself enjoy beautiful dreams of your bright, vibrant future, filled with opportunities for health and harmony, joy and vitality.*

Emerging: *If this is a time for you to be awake, alert and even conscious, then you can begin the process of coming back into the room. When you are ready to feel physically good for no apparent reason, when you are ready to see through new eyes from better and healthier perspectives, then at that moment your eyes will open. You will be wide awake! Wide awake! Feeling fine and in perfect health! And this is so!*

If you are working on sleep with a client (see chapter 7), you might want to reverse the order on your recording — putting the emerging first, and then quickly moving in to the deepener, with the goal of providing the option to leave the person asleep as she or he listens to the recording.

Incidentally, it is not possible to be "stuck" in hypnosis. Hypnosis is simply a relaxed state. A hypnotized person will either emerge (or awaken) or fall into actual Delta sleep, and then eventually awaken.

For subjects who are more difficult to emerge, consider a tap on the toe (for clients who are in a recliner) or a tap on the shoulder.

5 RAPID INDUCTIONS & HYPNOTIC DEPTH

"You're a hypnotist, really? No!" We had just met at an art gallery opening, beginning with a little chit-chat about a painting. I asked what she did—and then she asked what I did.

"Hey, would I kid you about a thing like that?" We bantered a little bit, and I asked her if she had any questions about hypnosis. When it was obvious that she was intrigued, I dropped the suggestion: "You know, if you like, I could drop you into a wonderful relaxed state, right here, right now."

She continued to engage, and I could tell she was considering it. It was a safe place—lots of people around, lots of noise. She was with a friend, and so was I.

"Hey, if you can't trust a random guy you've just met at an art gallery, who can you trust?" I offered with a smile. "How often do you have a chance to really enjoy the experience of hypnosis from a professional hypnotist. There's no time like the present!"

She was intrigued and decided to go with it—and two minutes later she was under; it was a great experience for her.

Not much is more impressive than a rapid induction—dropping someone into a deeply relaxed state in 20 or 30 seconds, while she or he is standing up in the middle of a noisy party. These are not just party tricks, though, and there is a lot about hypnosis to be learned from this section of the book, even if you don't decide to do rapid inductions.

Remember, pacing and leading are important. The induction begins with the waking state interaction, so the whole process is really longer than the seemingly instant drop-down into a hypnotic state.

Be open and friendly in both verbal and nonverbal communication. A nice smile and a little self-deprecation don't hurt: "It's almost like I know what I'm doing!" There is no point in forcing the issue with someone who is hesitant. Begin by developing "yes sets," or compliance. Ask questions or make statements you know your subject will answer, "yes;" nod as you talk.

Okay, this is going to be great fun, right? You will really enjoy this, you know. So the first thing is that if you were a client in my office, I'd have a comfy recliner, nice music, and I'd take about five minutes to talk you into a wonderful, comfortable, peaceful relaxed state. This will be nothing like that!

(This almost always gets a laugh; at the least, it will confuse, which is also good.)

Also, if you were a client I would not touch you, but to do this, I need to be able to touch you on the arm or shoulder – would that be okay?

Permission to touch the subject is critical. While most hypnotic processes do not involve any touching, you will need to do this to do a rapid induction. Never touch someone without her or his permission. Remember your professional ethic—you have been given permission to touch the arm or shoulder, so don't wander far afield.

You might also end up touching the person's head or face. Some cultural groups may be very hesitant about this. Know who you are working with.

You also need to determine if you will do the rapid induction while the subject is standing or sitting. Sitting is nice if it is an option. Just use two chairs facing each other, so you and the subject are knee to knee.

Things become a little more complex if you are standing. First, don't do this with anyone who is so big (tall, heavy) that you couldn't catch them. I will only do standing rapid inductions with women and small men. Be ready!

Your subject's safety is your first priority. If standing, be sure to suggest, *"You will be steady on your feet the entire time."*

As you move into this process you must project absolute confidence. You will not be using a script. Just be sure you have the general pattern in your mind.

Create compliance by asking the subject to step slightly to one side or the other, or to move forward or back in the chair. If sitting, you want her or him to be sitting forward on the seat, but not so far that she or he might fall off.

Move with confidence through the process.

Okay, I'm just going to take your arm, and I'd like you to let your arm be loose and limp, like a limp rubber band, like all the muscles have just melted away.

Gently shake the subject's arm. If she or he keeps the arm stiff or somewhat stiff, she or he may not be the best subject. Continue to explain and suggest having a loose, limp arm.

This begins to take us to the core of rapid inductions: Rapid inductions are a variety of confusion induction in which a moment of social meaninglessness or confusion is created. The person does not have a social pattern or response for what you are doing (having someone shake your arm is not a normal behavior). It results in what is known as a transderivational search: The subject is mentally seeing some kind of social norm to play in this situation, and cannot find one. Once the confusion is created, you will take advantage of the disorientation by filling it with a suggestion to SLEEP! Then move immediately into suggestions to deepen the hypnotic state.

As your arm is so loose and limp [continue shaking it gently], *I'd like to invite you to watch my fingers*

Begin wiggling your fingers in front of the subject's eyes (being careful, of course, not to touch his or her eyes or face). I usually go back and forth and up, sort of like an upside down T, but the exact motion does not matter.

Watch your subject's eyes. If they flutter or glaze, you are in. Either way, after saying strongly:

Watch my fingers! Watch my fingers! Follow my fingers with your eyes!

Say, strongly and confidently,

SLEEP!

Drop your hand, drop the subject's arm with your other hand, and gently tap the person on the back of her or his neck with the hand which was holding his or her arm. Do not force the subject's head forward. Just give a very gentle tap.

Continue to say *SLEEP! SLEEP! SLEEP!*

You will need to IMMEDIATELY and confidently move into deepeners—suggestions to deepen the hypnotic state. A patter something like this works:

Deepener: *Going deeper, deeper, deeper now, more relaxed and more comfortable. Each breath takes you deeper, each word takes you deeper. Drifting, dreaming floating, flowing, calm, relaxed, completely at peace. Each time I lift and drop your arm you go deeper!* [Do it and keep doing it]. *Each time I say SLEEP! you go deeper. SLEEP! Calm, relaxed, completely at peace! And I wonder if you would like to double or triple your level of relaxation. I wonder if you would like to double or even triple the relaxation you feel in your neck and shoulders, or if you would like to try to keep that stress a little longer while other parts of your body relax first. SLEEP! Noticing how heavy your eyes are becoming, your eyes which are so heavy it begins to feel if they are glued shut. Deeper now! SLEEP!* etc.

Other Ideas for Rapid Inductions

Any motion which does not have a social context will work as a rapid induction. It does not matter how you move your hands or the subject's hands; the entire process is in the suggestions you've made, primarily leading up to the rapid induction. Above is a process of moving fingers in front of the subject's eyes. Here are some other ideas. All these require the setup beforehand (pacing, leading, yes sets, permission, etc.)

The handshake rapid induction. Reach for the subject's right hand with your right hand, as if to shake hands. As he or she reaches for your hand, suddenly grab her or his hand with your left hand, pull the arm, and say firmly *SLEEP!* Move immediately and confidently into deepeners.

Press my hand rapid induction. I usually use this one to take a person down again, once a previous rapid induction has been done. Standing face to face, place your right hand, palm up, stomach height. Ask the subject to put her or his hand on your hand and press down as hard as he or she can. Look deeply into her or his eyes and say, forcefully, *Press harder, harder—C'mon, you can do better than that!* Suddenly yank your right hand away, causing him or her to become unbalanced. Close your eyes as you do this (as a cue to the subject to close her or his eyes), and then open your eyes immediately. Gently tap the back of his or her neck with your left hand. Move immediately and confidently into deepeners.

Falling leaves rapid induction. Hold the subject's left forearm with your right hand, and tell her or him to make it loose and limp. Say, *Imagine your arm is a heavy tree limb, just swaying in the wind. I'll hold it up, just let your arm go limp. Gently swaying in the wind. Your fingers are like leaves of the tree—just keep your eyes locked on the leaves,* [stroke the fingers briefly with your left hand], *follow your fingers with your eyes, gentle leaves.* Shake his or her fingers in front of his or her eyes. You should notice the arm getting heavy, and perhaps the eyes glazing. Suddenly drop the arm and say firmly and confidently *SLEEP!* Move immediately and confidently into deepeners.

Swinging watch rapid induction. I love this one! It plays off the traditional swinging watch induction, and involves the same cheat in that the eyes get fatigued; as a bonus, the arm may become fatigued as well. Again, you can use a pendant, crystal, necklace, or any such object. If you borrow her necklace, be sure to find out who she wants you to hand it to while she is under. Say, *I'm going to let you be the hypnotist. Hold this watch in front of your eyes, and let it gently swing* [two to four inches in front of the eyes, swinging about the width of the eyes, to keep the hand from being up too high]. As the subject swings the watch, say, *Your eyes are getting heavy, you're getting sleepy.* Then suddenly say *SLEEP!* and gently knock the subject's hand down. Immediately go into a deepener.

6 HYPNOTIC SUGGESTIBILITY: THE ARON'S DEPTH SCALE

Hypnotic depth is essentially a behavioral assessment of how hypnotized someone is; it's a different concept from the Beta, Alpha, Theta, and Delta relaxation levels we looked at earlier. Several standards exist for measuring hypnotic susceptibility (also termed suggestibility or depth); one of these, the Food and Drug Administration (FDA) approved Bispectral Index Scale, measures brain wave cycles (Johansen and Sebel, 2000). Other well-known scales, based on behavioral assessments, are the Stanford Hypnotic Susceptibility Scale, Form C (Weitzenhoffer, Hilgard, and Kihlstrom, 1962) and the Harvard Group Scale of Hypnotic Susceptibility, Form A (Shor and Orne, 1962). The most widely used scale is the Arons Master Depth Rule, often called the "Arons Scale" (Arons, 1961). Harry Arons proposed six levels of suggestibility:

Level One: Small muscle catalepsy—the subject tries but cannot open the eyes.

Level Two: Large muscle catalepsy—the subject tries but cannot move a major muscle group. This could range from arm rigidity to full body rigidity. Important note: Hypnosis does not impart super-human powers. Some stage hypnotists have induced full body rigidity, and then stood upon their subjects. There are tricks to doing this "properly," which I will not divulge, but this is inherently dangerous and should not be attempted under any circumstances. Remember, your first duty is the safety of your subject.

Interestingly, Cojan, et al. (two studies, both published in 2009) provided neuroimaging or brain scan studies demonstrating how hypnotic catalepsy or paralysis works. Essentially, the muscles of the body can be operated by different sections of the brain. Catalepsy results when an other-than-conscious part of the brain creates rigidity; this other-than-conscious signal prevents signals from the conscious mind (or executive function) from reaching and operating the muscles. Picture a railroad track with a train on it. Another train cannot get on the track since the track is full. Likewise, with hypnotic catalepsy, the muscle is locked out and cannot be moved.

Non-REM (Rapid Eye Movement) sleep paralysis is a similar phenomenon, and is actually an important safety function of the body; it keeps you from acting out your dreams and injuring yourself or your sleeping partner. However, waking and experiencing this paralysis can be very disturbing. People experiencing paralysis—a parasomnia disorder—upon awakening from sleep often report hallucinations; they feel an ominous or demonic presence either in the room or sitting on top of them, holding them down and trying to suffocate them. Fortunately, hypnosis provides an effective way to reframe these night terror or sleep terror experiences.

Level Three: Analgesia: In the presence of painful stimuli (such as a pinch), the subject feels touch or pressure, but no pain. This also applies to memory; the subject can think of an answer to a question (as reported after the hypnosis process) but cannot say it. For example, told "Try to say your name, but you cannot," the subject would not be able to say her or his name, although afterward he or she would report being able to recall it.

Level Four: Anesthesia—in the presence of painful stimuli, the subject feels nothing. More will be said on this in the chapter on pain alleviation. Remember, however, that although the subject does not experience pain, the body can still be damaged. Keep your subject safe. Memory is also affected; at Level Four, the subject neither recalls nor can state the information.

Level Five: Positive hallucination: The subject experiences (sees, hears, smells, or feels) phenomena which are not actually present. For example the subject thinks he or she can see and can describe an ornate clock on a wall that is actually blank.

Level Six: Negative hallucination: The subject does not experience something which is actually, physically present. For example, the person does not see a pen on the table before her or him, feels barefoot even though he or she is wearing shoes, or does not understand why she or he is sitting in air once the supporting chair has "vanished."

It is important to note that suggestibility does not correlate with effectiveness. Almost all significant clinical work can be done at Level One (obviously, anesthesia requires greater depth). But hypnosis is the art of suggestion, and emotionally suggestive language can be used at any of the levels of consciousness, not just when the subject is "under" in a hypnotic state.

The Arons levels have limited usefulness in clinical hypnosis, but are fun to observe when combined with rapid or other inductions in a party or street hypnosis situation.

Script: Hypnotic Depth
This is not an induction; it is a hypnotic process. Once you have done any sort of induction you can transition into this process to assess hypnotic suggestibility. I tend to move into this from the deeper of the rapid inductions.

[Deepener:] *Going deeper, deeper, deeper now, more relaxed and more comfortable. Each breath takes you deeper, each word takes you deeper. Drifting, dreaming floating, flowing, calm relaxed, completely at peace. Each time I lift and drop your arm you go deeper!* [Do it and keep doing it]. *Each time I say SLEEP! you go deeper. SLEEP! Calm, relaxed, completely at peace! And I wonder if you would like to double or triple your level of relaxation. I wonder if you would like to double or even triple the relaxation you feel in your neck and shoulders, or if you would like to try to keep that stress a little longer while other parts of your body relax first. SLEEP!*

[Level One:] *Noticing how heavy your eyes are becoming, your eyes which are so heavy it begins to feel if they are glued shut. In fact you find that you can try to open your eyes and you cannot and you go deeper now! You try and you cannot and you go deeper now!*

[Level Two:] *But that's not important right now. Of course your body will only move in ways that are comfortable and appropriate for you. What's important is to realize you are a strong, confident man/woman. This time as I lift your arm you will find that your arm becomes stiff and rigid, like a steel beam, an iron bar.*

[Lift the arm; gently pull it straight. You may want to turn the arm, gently, so that the bend of the elbow is down and the wrist is up. This makes it a little easier to lock in place. The arm may be rigid, but may not stay up if you let go. If you realize this is the case, continue to support the arm.]

If at any level the suggestions are not taken, do an emerging. Thank the subject for working with you. Tell him or her, "You did a great job with this! Hypnosis is measured on a one to six scale, one is lightest and six is deepest. In this setting we got you to a level two (or another level), which was fine. Different people can be hypnotized in different ways. In another setting, using another approach, you may go deeper. Thank you for letting me do this with you. You were great!"

It is important to have an escape path. This will give you confidence in trying rapid inductions. Remember, you never fail and the client never fails. Create a narrative of success, no matter what happens. Also, never tell someone that she or he can't be hypnotized—that is simply not true.

If the person passes level two, at this point I usually emerge him or her, and then do another rapid induction. This is a process of *fractionation*—taking someone down, then up, then down again in order to increase hypnotic depth.

Great! Coming back into the room, back into the room, feeling great!

I usually touch him or her on the shoulder as I say this, as a cue for emerging.

Continuing straight on, rapidly: *You were great! That was fun. Now look into my eyes and press on my hand. Harder! Harder! SLEEP!*

Level Three (or Four): *Deeper now, drifting dreaming floating flowing, calm relaxed completely at peace. Each time I tell you to sleep you go deeper. Each time I lift and drop your arm you go deeper, now. Each word takes you deeper, each number takes you deeper. 10, 9, 8, 7, 5, 4, 3, 2, 1 – deeper!* [Notice the number 6 is omitted] *But that's not important right now. What's important is how good your hands feel.*

[Place the subject's hands in her or his lap or simply say, *your hand will simply float in the air, here!* as you place the subject's hand in the air at about waist height (note—not above the heart, as that will create a strain). Begin touching fingers as you count, leaving out the number 6].

Each number takes you deeper! 10, 9, 8, 7, 5, 4, 3, 2, 1! The number 6 is gone from your thoughts, gone from your mind, gone from your body's awareness. You might be able to think it but you simply can't say it. Deeper! 10, 9, 8, 7, 5, 4, 3, 2, 1. Now coming back into the room, back into the room! [Tap the shoulder and emerge the subject for fractionation. Keep going, rapidly. You may notice the subject's eyes glazing as he or she is "awake."]

Now count with me [touching fingers] *10, 9, 8, 7 SLEEP!* [At this point a simple, gentle tap on the forehead should take the subject under as an impressive rapid induction. Keep going!]

Deeper now! 10, 9, 8, 7, 5, 4, 3, 2, 1! The number 6 vanishes away, gone from your thoughts, your mind, your body's awareness. It just vanishes, just like your name, your name which vanishes away, gone from your thoughts, your mind, your body's awareness. You might be able to think it but you cannot say it. 10, 9, 8, 7, 5, 4, 3, 2, 1! Deeper! Sleep! Wide awake! Eyes wide open! [Tap the shoulder.]

Now count with me, 10, 9, 8, 7, now try to tell me your name. Try and you cannot! SLEEP! [Gently tap the subject's forehead.] *And deeper!*

Then actually let the subject count fingers. See if he or she misses the number six. If so, you can try asking questions like "what is 3+3?" If the wrong answer is given, you might try suggesting something like, *The answer to all math questions is 47! 47 is the answer to all math questions. It feels so good to say it! 47!*

Then emerge the person and see if 3+3=47. Quickly re-induce hypnosis by saying *SLEEP!* and gently tapping the forehead.

If the subject cannot say her or his name, you can suggest something like, *Your name is Susan! Susan is your name!* [assuming, of course that her name is not Susan—if it is, then pick something else.] Emerge and ask, *What's your name?*

Level Five: *SLEEP! Deeper now, so relaxed and so comfortable! You notice that you have the most beautiful blonde hair* [use this suggestion if the subject is brunette, or vice versa]—*it cascades around your shoulders. The more you tell me about it the better you will feel!*

Or: *You are wearing the most gorgeous dress* [if the subject is wearing a shirt and pants]—*feel the texture of the fabric, so comfortable. It is your favorite color!* Emerge the subject and ask him or her, "What color is your hair? How long is it? How does it feel? or What color is the dress? How long is it? What is the neckline like? and so forth.

Remember, if at any point the subject does not take the suggestions, thank him or her for doing this, explain the levels, and let him or her know that in another setting she or he may go deeper. Re-hypnotize the subject (*SLEEP!* finger tap on forehead) and take away all suggestions (see below), even if she or he seems like they are totally "up."

Level Six: *You notice that your feet are getting colder and colder; in fact, you are barefoot. Even with that beautiful gown, barefoot! Someone here has your shoes, and you need to find them. You won't do anything violent, but you may ask for your shoes. Back in the room, eyes open!* [shoulder tap].

At the end of your demonstration, wrap it up and close all the loops—that is, eliminate all suggestions. Re-hypnotize the subject (*SLEEP!* finger tap on forehead) and say, *You had a great time with this! You will remember everything that's happened, and you really enjoyed it! Your clothes are back to normal, you know your name and the number six, your feet are comfortable and your shoes are on. You can let go of all those silly suggestions. You will feel refreshed and very good. It may be that there is something you've been trying to accomplish in your life, and your powerful creative side can help you with that now. Back in the room! Eyes wide open! Wide awake!* [Tap shoulder].

You could also try a post-hypnotic suggestion, such as, *You will still have that beautiful blonde hair until you walk out of this room, then you will know your hair returns to normal—and your normal hair is beautiful!* Otherwise, close all loops. This is important, even if the person seems "up." People can feel vague emotional discomfort for a short time as a result of suggestions left open.

Also, it is likely that the subject will remember everything, even without a suggestion to remember. Hypnotic amnesia is notoriously unreliable, even if you suggest it. You cannot count on amnesia, and you should always treat your subjects with respect and dignity. Leave people feeling good about themselves, like they performed as the stars of the show. Remember to give a brief description of the levels and what happened, and thank the subject for being a good sport.

7 SLEEP!

A Bit of Hypno History

When Dr. James Braid coined the terms *hypnotism* and *hypnotized* in 1842 to describe the state of relaxed suggestibility, he almost immediately regretted doing it.

Braid proposed the terms as alternatives for "animal magnetism" or mesmerism. Franz Anton Mesmer believed in "animal magnetism" not as a metaphor for being attractive to someone of the opposite sex, but as an actual physical energy or magnetic "fluid" in the body. Mesmer attributed changes as a result of his process—mesmerism—to changes in this "magnetic fluid."

Mesmer became interested in "magnetism" through the work of Father Maximilian Hell (probably the best priest name ever), a Jesuit priest, who performed exorcisms using an iron cross. Mesmer concluded that the key to Hell's success was the iron, which manipulated the magnetic fluid of the body. This concept of healing through the manipulation of mysterious and empirically unmeasurable magnetic or energy fields in the body continues to the present day—for instance in the concept of manipulating Chi (or Qi) energy, Reiki, or buying copper or magnetic bracelets as a cure for arthritis.

Mesmer was a flamboyant showman who had a penchant for wearing gold slippers and lilac silk robes and conducted his sessions in a séance-like atmosphere. His personal style created the caricature of the charlatan. He came to fame in Vienna as a result of "curing" the hysterical blindness of Maria Theresia von Paradis, a member of the court of Holy Roman Empress Maria Theresa and friend of composer Wolfgang Amadeus Mozart (who once performed a concert on Mesmer's back yard). Apparently Mesmer's tête-à-têtes with the 18-year-old Paradis were not entirely ethical, and he was forced to flee Vienna and relocate in Paris in 1778 (after which Paradis' blindness returned).

Mesmer became so popular in Paris that he treated large numbers of patients at the same time. Dr. John Grieve, a British physician, noted that Mesmer never treated fewer than 200 patients at a time. Grieve describes what he saw at Mesmer's home in May of 1784:

> In the middle of the room is placed a vessel of about a foot and a half high which is called here a baquet. It is so large that twenty people can easily sit round it; near the edge of the lid which covers it, there are holes pierced corresponding to the number of persons who are to surround it; into these holes are introduced iron rods, bent at right angles outwards, and of different heights, so as to answer to the part of the body to which they are to be applied. Besides these rods, there is a rope which communicates between the baquet and one of the patients, and from him is carried to another, and so on the whole round. The most sensible effects are produced on the approach of Mesmer, who is said to convey the fluid by certain motions of his hands or eyes, without touching the person. I have talked with several who have witnessed these effects, who have convulsions occasioned and removed by a movement of the hand. (Ellenberger, 1970, p. 63)

Students of hypnosis will recognize the baquet and the iron rods which were bent to touch the afflicted part of the body as hypnotic anchoring, or the association of an emotional suggestion with a physical sensation (we will look at anchoring as a means of heading off migraine headaches in Chapter 8). Everyone should recognize this as an example of the placebo effect.

French king Louis XVI was skeptical of Mesmer. In 1784 he appointed a Royal Commission to investigate the scientific basis for mesmerism. The commission was headed by American ambassador to France Benjamin Franklin, and included Antoine Lavoisier, the father of modern chemistry, floral botanist Antoine Laurent de Jussieu, and Joseph-Ignace Guillotin (not the inventor of the guillotine).

The Franklin Commission performed several experiments, including one in which a tree at Franklin's residence in Passy was "magnetized" by Charles d'Eslon, an associate of Mesmer. A blindfolded subject was asked to identify the tree—and could not (he fainted). The commission found that there was no basis for animal magnetism or magnetic fluid, although de Jussieu wrote a dissenting report. The commission found that mesmerism produced cures through suggestion, imagination, or charlatanry.

Although mesmerism was discredited by the Franklin Commission Report, debate about the power of the process to create change continued, and the negative publicity even boosted the fame of mesmerism.

Braid was interested in a serious study of the phenomena and wanted to get away from the charlatan-like trappings and reputation of mesmerism. He coined terms related to the Greck word for sleep, hypnos, even though he realized the process did not involve actual sleep. Although Braid only saw sleep as a metaphor for the relaxation process, the association of hypnosis with sleep has become iconic. Unfortunately the image of a tux and tails stage hypnotist intoning "Sleep!" to a busty swooning woman has continued to associate hypnosis with charlatanism, and the process continues to be stigmatized.

For some time, serious behavioral scientists studying or using the phenomena have used other terminology like functional relaxation or guided imagery. Serious modern psychological and neurological studies of the phenomena have begun to use the term hypnosis more prevalently, and as noted in Chapter 1 the basis of the relaxation process is now very well understood.

Baquet and Brain Scans

As for the baquet, Judson (2010, para 1) notes: "The placebo effect is, potentially, one of the most powerful forces in medicine." The neurological basis of the placebo effect is becoming much more well understood. Benedetti, Mayberg, Wager, Stohler, and Zubieta (2005) demonstrate that the brain makes a distinct chemical response when patients are given a treatment they expect to work: "Any medical treatment is surrounded by a psychosocial context that affects the therapeutic outcome" (p. 10390).

The power of this mental framing effect can be seen in a number of ways. Kirsch, Moore, Scoboria, and Nicholls (2002) found that suggestive or placebo effects accounted for approximately 80 percent of the efficacy of the six most widely prescribed antidepressants approved by the FDA between 1987 and 1999. Hart, Ksir, and Ray (2009, p. 105) note, "A good 'trip' or a bad trip on LSD seems to be more dependent on the experiences and mood of the user before taking the drug than on the amount or quality of the drug taken." Ray (2004) describes the dramatic effect mental framing and suggestion have on healing the body:

> From the biopsychosocial perspective, the mind is one activity of the brain, and this activity of the brain is the body's first line of defense against illness, against aging, against death, and for health and well-being. The concepts and facts I cover below are not ephemeral but are based in biochemistry, physiology, and neuroanatomy. Several years ago, Norman Cousins used the phrase "belief becomes biology." That is certainly true. We know that our beliefs influence the biology of our bodies. When an experience is psychological, not physical, it is all in the mind. However, because the mind is a part of the functioning brain, the body responds to the brain regardless of whether the beliefs and ideas are imaginary or based in reality, or whether they are positive or negative. What a person thinks does make a difference—sometimes it is good for him or her, sometimes it is bad. (p. 32)

The baquet had important lessons to teach, which were lost in Mesmer's flurry of purple silk and showmanship. Modern neuroscience is now unfolding the empirical effects which were unfortunately beyond what Franklin and his commission could imagine in 1784.

Hypnosis for Sleep
Even though hypnosis is not sleep, it is a relaxation process. While hypnosis provides a powerful tool for changing conscious behavior, sleep behaviors are clearly not under cognitive control, so hypnotic relaxation is an even more obvious tool to use to change sleep behaviors.

Sleep is a serious issue. In 2013 the U.S. Centers for Disease Control and Prevention (CDC) published an article titled "Insufficient Sleep Is a Public Health Epidemic," and stated:

> Sleep is increasingly recognized as important to public health, with sleep insufficiency linked to motor vehicle crashes, industrial disasters, and medical and other occupational errors. Unintentionally falling asleep, nodding off while driving, and having difficulty performing daily tasks because of sleepiness all may contribute to these hazardous outcomes. Persons experiencing sleep insufficiency are also more likely to suffer from chronic diseases such as hypertension, diabetes, depression, and obesity, as well as from cancer, increased mortality, and reduced quality of life and productivity. ("Insufficient," 2013)

In a popular article in *The New York Times*, Thakkar (2013) noted that sleep deficits are strongly associated with attention deficit hyperactivity disorder (ADHD), and may well be the real issue in addressing problems of focus.

As noted in Chapter 1, awareness, relaxation and sleep are a continuum. Going to sleep is not simply like throwing an on/off switch. It is more like turning down a dimmer switch. Additionally, the depth of relaxation varies throughout the sleep cycles, so there are periods when someone is more or less asleep. Additionally, people tend to think that it takes some period of time to go to sleep.

However, as noted in the discussion of rapid inductions in Chapter 5, it is possible for someone to move from a completely awake state into a deep level of relaxation very quickly, in just a few seconds. Since relaxation has to do with the electric brain wave cycle, this is not surprising. Electricity moves very quickly!

The following process is designed to help someone sleep deeply at night. For fun, I have also included suggestions for lucid dreaming. Lucid dreaming occurs when one enters a light state of relaxation or sleep, is somewhat aware of dreaming, and can then change the course of the dream. This can be very helpful for dealing with nightmares, and it can be a lot of fun just in general.

Script: Deep, Restful Sleep
Any induction will do, but the Progressive Relaxation with Ego Strengtheners in Chapter 4 is a great lead-in for this process.

Just continuing to relax deeply, and as you are so calm, so relaxed, so completely at peace, you can begin to notice just how good, just how relaxed you feel. I wonder what it would feel like if you were to double or triple that comfortable relaxation. I wonder if you can imagine what it would feel like if you were as relaxed as you can possibly be. So now you can just take a few deep breaths, with each breath deeper, more comfortable, sleep.

And each night as you fall asleep you will be calm, at ease, relaxed. The thoughts of the day just seem to chase away, like autumn leaves scattered by a pleasant wind, just beyond your grasp, and you can simply let them go, let them flow.

As your head touches your pillow and you pull your sheets or blanket over you, snuggling in so peacefully, this is your cue to enter a deep, restful, comfortable sleep. So relaxed, so comfortable, so completely at peace. Have you ever seen a small child just sprawled out asleep, or a cat or dog just snuggled down for a nap? Not a care in the world, completely at peace. You will let yourself sleep that way, deeply, comfortably.

Of course some people think it takes a while to go to sleep, but you can just while away the time and waft into a deep sleep right away. Your brain flows in electric cycles, slower and deeper as you relax, let go, drift off, sleep. And how long does it take to turn down a dimmer switch? A light that is bright and glowing, a hundred watts, and you can just watch the watts drop with a flick of the fingers, turning the dimmer switch down immediately to the soft, beige, comfortable 40-watt mellow glow. It is that fast, just like flicking a switch, to dream to flow to go.

And part of you knows just how powerful this sleep is. This is the time when your body is cleansing itself, letting go of the toxins which have built up in the cells during the movement of the day, focusing the body's healing power—50 million cells a second, changing and rearranging in just the right sequence and order for you—creating healing in your body.

And there is a part of you that knows that this is your time to create, to flow. As you let go now, letting the conscious mind simply skip away to play in the garden of your subconscious thoughts, there is a powerful other-than-conscious part of you—a part of you which sees connections which you didn't see consciously, a creative part of you which sees options and solutions. We all know that we can create better when we sleep on it, and this super conscious part of you is creating now.

So you can let go because your subconscious is always there, always taking care of you. It is okay to flow because your superconscious is creating. Your sleep can be the most productive part of your day!

Even now your powerful other-than-conscious is focused on the things which are truly important in your life, not merely the things which seem to be urgent. This creative part of you is focused on your priorities, the goals to reach your priorities, the action steps to reach your goals. Soon taking action and accomplishing goals will become second nature for you—imagine that. And you can let go now, going deeper now, so sleepy now, because I wonder just what you will discover. I wonder what treasure your subconscious will give you when you wake in the morning, refreshed and renewed, seeing through new eyes from better and healthier perspectives, ready for a wonderful day.

So this is your time to sleep deeply, to renew, to create. Sleeping so deeply that outside sounds and influences only carry you deeper. If there were ever an emergency you would awaken immediately knowing what to do, because your subconscious is on the lookout, taking care of you, so you can let go, sleep, flow, as you trust that part of yourself to let you sleep deeply now.

And even if you are roused during the night, perhaps to go to the bathroom, you will find that you can just return quickly, quietly to bed. As your head touches your pillow and you pull the sheets or blankets over you, this is your cue to fall into a deep, refreshing, dreamy sleep. Sleeping so deeply and comfortably through the night that you won't even recall that you were ever roused. This will be the one thing you cannot remember. The more you try to remember the more difficult it will be. Simply remembering to forget by forgetting to remember you will awaken refreshed, feeling that you have slept deeply through the night.

Dreaming beautiful dreams. Now I don't know if you'd rather dream dreams of your bright, vibrant future. Or you might want to dream dreams of the things you are doing to create your future and your life and world. Or you might just like to dream of a fantasy of a place so comfortable and relaxing that you can just let everything flow.

I wonder if you ever notice when you are dreaming. Sometimes people do—sleeping in such a light state that it seems like there is a bit of awareness I'm in a dream. And psychologists call that lucid dreaming—dreaming a dream where you can steer the dream, taking the dream-story to places you want to go, like your own movie or novel in your mind. And I wonder what novel things you will enjoy as you carry your dreams to beautiful places. Even difficult dreams can be steered in the most joyous, luxurious, delightful directions. So I wonder how much you are going to enjoy sleeping deeply now.

The mind drifts, the thoughts scatter, this is your time to create without knowing it, to refresh, to renew. This can be some of the best time of your day, so let it flow.

And in the morning when you awaken, you will be refreshed, renewed, invigorated, looking forward to the day. You will feel so good, filled with energy, with the joy of living! As you waken in the morning part of you will know exactly what to do to make the most of your day, so you can look forward to awakening, feeling refreshed, feeling renewed, feeling good!

If this is a time when you need to be awake, refreshed, up and going, then you can begin to come back into the room. When you are ready to feel physically good for no apparent reason at all, when you are ready to see through new eyes, from better and healthier perspectives, then at that moment your eyes will open—wide awake feeling fine!

If this is a time for you to be sleeping, then there is a part of you which has already begun the journey into deep restful sleep. As your head touches the pillow and you pull the sheets or blankets over you, you let yourself flow into a deep, dreaming restful sleep. Dreaming beautiful dreams of your bright, joyous future, and knowing that every day in every way your life is getting better, your world is getting better, and this is so.

Notice the fun reversal of the emerging at the end of this process. Since this is a sleep process, it makes sense to end with suggestions for sleep, particularly if you are recording this for your client. Since the emerging involves taking the client up and then going deeper immediately after, this takes advantage of fractionation to take the client deeper into sleep.

8 PHYSICAL PAIN ALLEVIATION

On September 11, 2001, shortly after hearing that the South Tower of the World Trade Center collapsed, I stood up from my desk and experienced riveting pain, unlike anything I'd ever felt before. I later learned that I had a herniated disk in my lower back. It had nothing to do with the terrorist attacks, of course; this was the result of repetitive stress and poor ergonomics over a long period of time. Somehow I managed to drive myself to a chiropractor (for the first time ever), and then eventually I went to my doctor's office. I spent the rest of the day on pain killers, and I am sure I am one of the few Americans alive that day who doesn't remember watching the news coverage of those horrific attacks.

This was before my journey into hypnosis. That day led to nine months of conferring with doctors, consideration of surgery, and being pretty much confined to a sofa, chair, or bed. I was in so much pain that I could not stand to be on my feet long enough to go to the store. I thought my life would never be normal again. Eventually I found a pain management specialist who helped tremendously by giving me a steroid shot in the back. It took my pain to a much lower level, but I was still dealing with significant pain every day.

Then I discovered hypnotic pain alleviation, a process of creating physical numbness. I was able to use these processes to completely eliminate my back pain and dramatically improve my life. I do know that my body has not been healed, and there are things I don't do because I want to avoid further injury.

In January 2007, my daughter was popping popcorn on our stove. Being naturally clumsy, somehow I managed to knock the saucepan and get my hand into the hot oil. The pain was immediate and intense. I quickly cooled the burn in running water, but my hand still hurt and appeared bright red.

I grabbed the hypnosis recordings that I had used years before to deal with my back pain. It took more than an hour of hypnosis for my hand to become numb, but after that it never hurt again, even though it appeared red for several weeks.

Of all the things I work on with clients, I have the most satisfaction when I am able to help them eliminate physical pain.

Chemical anesthetics are the legacy of Dr. James Young Simpson, a 19th century Scottish physician who discovered chloroform. Modern anesthesia is a tremendous blessing.

There are drawbacks to chemical anesthesia, however. In the early 1990s, the National Institutes of Health (NIH) was concerned about contraindications or conflicts between anesthetic drugs and chemotherapy medications. They investigated non-medical anesthesia processes—a variety of relaxation, breathing and meditation techniques, hypnosis, biofeedback, and Cognitive Behavior Therapy (CBT). The research found strong empirical evidence to support the use hypnosis in pain alleviation ("Integration," 1995).

This would not have surprised Dr. James Esdale, another Scottish physician and a contemporary of Dr. Simpson. While working in India, Dr. Esdale performed numerous surgeries using hypnosis as the only anesthesia—which was fortunate for his patients, since the alternatives at the time were beverage alcohol and biting on a piece of wood or leather.

Hypnosis has a long history of pain alleviation. In fact, it is this process which intrigued the journalist John

Stossel, a co-anchor of ABC News's *20/20*. In his book *Myths, Lies and Downright Stupidity*, Stossel described his experience watching a woman have eye surgery using hypnosis as the only anesthesia. He states, "Just when my skeptic's antennae convinced me I always know bunk when I see it, I get fooled. I assumed hypnosis in medicine was one more con game. Truth: Hypnosis works—if you let it!" (2007, p. 215).

The 1995 NIH report noted that the biological basis of hypnotic anesthesia was not understood. Thanks to advances in neuroimaging or bran scan technology, these processes are now very well understood. Using fMRI brain scans, Schulz-Stübner, et al. (2004) found that hypnotic processes interrupt pain signals from the body and prevent them from reaching the higher cortical structures of the brain, which are responsible for pain perception.

Hypnosis is the art of suggestion, even when it is not performed in a relaxed state. Placebo effects are best understood as suggestive or waking state hypnotic processes. It is important to understand that placebo changes are real changes; however, they are caused emotionally rather than biochemically (cf. Carlat, 2010; Judson, 2010; Ray, 2004). Zubieta, et al. (2001) found that subjects given a simple saline solution, presented as an anesthetic, experienced pain relief—and positron emission tomography (PET) brain scans showed that this experience was accompanied by changes in brain chemistry similar to those induced by chemical anesthetics.

Emotional set and setting is also critical in the development of pain sensation. In another fMRI study, Ploghaus, et al., (1999) found that the anticipation of pain activated brain regions adjacent to those responsible for pain perception, which indicated that a suggestive process like emotional dissociation may be an effective means of pain alleviation.

The emotional state of the brain also explains why the same injury is not the same injury; that is, why some people experience similar injuries very differently. Baliki, et al., (2012) found that chronic pain emerges as an emotional response to injury. This effect is so profound that researchers were able to predict with 85 percent certainty which subjects would experience chronic pain based on the interactions of two parts of the brain that are related to emotional and motivational behavior.

Since we now know that the emotional response of the brain to injury creates chronic pain, it is reasonable that emotional processes will provide relief for chronic pain.

In addition to fMRI and PET scans, cerebral blood flow (CBF) provides another means of scanning the brain. CBF examines how blood flows to different parts of the brain. Crawford, Gur, Skolnick, Gur, and Benson (1993) found changes in CBF resulting from hypnotic pain alleviation processes. Similarly, Faymonville, et al., (2003) found changes in CBF associated with the reduction of pain as a result of hypnotic processes.

Since migraine is generally associated with the constriction of blood vessels in the brain, it is not surprising that Hammond (2007) found hypnosis to be effective in alleviating migraine and other headaches.

Another benefit of hypnotic pain alleviation is decreased surgical recovery time. Montgomery, David, Winkel, Silverstein, and Bovbjerg (2002) found that surgical patients using hypnotic pain alleviation processes in addition to traditional anesthesia "had better outcomes than 89% of patients in control groups" (p. 1639).

Key Considerations for Pain Alleviation Hypnosis
Chronic pain should always be diagnosed by a physician before hypnotic pain alleviation is performed. Although you can numb the body with hypnosis, you are not healing the body physically. Pain is not inherently bad; it is the body's way of informing us that something is wrong. It is important for any medical problems to be properly addressed; you do not want to address strange or undiagnosed pain. Once chronic pain is understood, hypnotic processes are then appropriate. Be sure to tell your client that the process is anesthetic (not a cure), and that he or she must continue to avoid any activities which would result in further injury.

You can use any induction to lead the client into a hypnotic state. It is a good idea to add the words *comfort* or *comfortable* into the induction as many times as possible.

For headaches, you should avoid using a confusion induction unless your client is highly analytical and will not relax any other way. If you choose progressive relaxation, skip over the parts of the body which are hurting (or just mention them briefly as feeling *more comfortable*). You do not want to focus attention on the hurting part of the body.

If the pain is in the core of the body (chest, back, abdomen), you will want to emphasize how the extremities *feel very good* (but don't go the other way and move extremity pain into the core).

For headaches, I like to emphasize how good the feet feel as part of the hypnotic process. This is a distraction process. I also remind the client to consciously think of how good his or her feet feel at the end of the session.

Many migraine headache sufferers have some sort of precursor sensation that lets them know a headache is coming. If this is the case, use a hypnotic anchoring process to suggest that the sensation leads them to notice how good their feet feel, that blood is flowing to their feet, and so on.

The script below is appropriate for the relief of any sort of pain. Some special attention is given to migraines or other headaches.

Script: Beautiful Winterscape, for Migraine or Other Pain

Use any induction (see the considerations above), and then move into the process:

Going deeper now, more relaxed. And as we do this process you know that pain, discomfort is not bad or wrong, it is your body's way of letting you know that something needs attention. So as we move into this process, you are sure that you and your doctor understand this discomfort, and that this discomfort is no longer needed for the greater good, to safeguard your body. So you can just breathe deeply and let it go now. Just breathe it out and let it go.

And as you continue to breathe deeply, just let your mind drift, and imagine that you are walking through a beautiful winter place, like a ski resort, or the mountains in winter. The sky is a deep, cold winter blue. You can see your breath, so cold. Deep white cold snow covers the ground, the boughs of the evergreens, and you can hear the crunch of the snow as you walk. You can feel a cold wind touching your temples, making your head colder and colder and colder and colder, and more numb.

You come to a beautiful, cold mountain stream, and see that the water is crystal clear and cold. You can see ice forming around the rocks at the edge of the stream. You bend down and put your hand into the cold, cold water. I wonder just how cold, just how numb your hand is right now. You know, blood flow can be changed with hypnosis, and part of you knows that the blood is simply flowing away from that hand now.

Perhaps it flows to your feet. I wonder if you can feel how heavy, how comfortable your feet feel at this moment. How amazingly relaxed, as the toes and the arch of the foot melt together, as the heel and the ankle flow together. Just a moment ago you were unaware of your feet, but now you notice just how relaxed, just how comfortable, they feel.

You need to understand that you have an unconscious ability you can learn how to use, and that ability is the ability to turn off the feeling in an arm, a hand, your head your feet or any part of your body. It does not matter how you do this, or how your unconscious simply does it for you. The only thing that is important is that you know you can turn off feeling, as easily as throwing a switch, where something unknown happens, that allows you to disconnect.

Migraine is always caused by the blood vessels of the brain becoming swollen and enlarged. You can imagine right now those swollen vessels. What happens if you simply allow all that blood to flow right now to your feet, if you really let yourself experience just how good, how comfortable your feet feel right now? Imagine the vessels of the head being soothed and smoothed and healed and comforted, returning to their natural, normal size and color. Feel that cold touching the temples, making the vessels of the head become smaller and more normal and oh so comfortable, as you focus on your feet, now.

You know, it may be that in the past you felt some sensation in your body that told you a migraine was coming. What would it be like if, when you felt that, you simply took in a deep, relaxing breath, all the way down to the diaphragm, and then slowly let it out as you allowed yourself to just become more and more aware of your feet, of how comfortable your feet feel? What would happen if you just let it go, let it flow, and let yourself feel comfortable as that sensation now reminds you of just how good your feet can possibly feel? How good would it feel if you imagine the blood vessels of the brain becoming soothed and comfortable even as you imagine the wonderful, comfortable warmth of your blood flowing to your feet?

You might notice just how comfortably numb your body is right now, as you continue to imagine walking through that beautiful winterscape, so cold and so numbing. Until you come to your lodge or cabin—it is so beautiful. As you step in you feel comfortable, relaxed. It feels good to prepare and slip into a comfortable, warm bath. As you sit in the bath, notice that the water covers your entire body, except for your head. As you turn on the faucet to make the water hotter and hotter, your temples feel colder and colder. When you are ready, you can pull the plug, and allow all the water, and any remaining discomfort, to drain out, and as you realize now just how comfortable, just how renewed, just how refreshed you feel.

[Emerging:] As you are listening to my voice, noticing just how good, just how comfortable you feel right now, in a moment I'm going to invite you to come back into this room, into this place. As you come back into the room you feel refreshed, renewed, energized, bringing with you a feeling of energy and joy and peace. Your hands feel good, your feet feel good! Coming back into the room, feeling wide awake, feeling fine and in perfect health! Eyes open! Wide awake! Feeling very, very good! And this is so!

[Awake:] You feel good! How do you feel?

Script: Garden Walk—Converting Discomfort to Another Modality

By definition, pain is kinesthetic—a body experience. It can help to convert that discomfort to another sensory modality, that is to make it visual or auditory. This metaphor is designed to do just that. You can use any induction:

And as you are going deeper now, so relaxed and comfortable, noticing how comfortable you are and perhaps wondering just how good you can feel, I'd like to invite you to imagine you are comfortably walking along in a beautiful place, like a lovely green garden. The sunlight is dappling the ground through the green leaves, and the shade feels so cool and wonderful. Your body moves easily, fluidly, comfortably. Perhaps a pleasant brook babbles beside your path, and you can notice all the shades of green leaves, gently rustling in the cool breeze.

As you consider those shades of green, I wonder what greens you are imagining right now. There can be so many. Perhaps your powerful other than conscious mind focuses on a bright kelly green, or a deep forest green, or even a light almost yellow spring green. I wonder if you can imagine those greens in your mind, and then comfortably shift the colors in your mind from one to another. I wonder if your powerful other than conscious can do that—perhaps starting with that light yellow-green, and then shifting it to darker and darker shades until it becomes a deep olive, then almost fades to black.

Or could you start with a dark forest green, and imagine it fading into lighter and lighter hues until it fades to that light yellow green which is almost white?

Never mind, that's not important right now. What is important is just how easily your body moves along this path beside the babbling stream. Notice how deep and rhythmic your breathing is, the deep sense of comfort and peace you feel.

As you walk along, so easily, effortlessly, you notice a lovely pebble beside the path. As you take the pebble in your hand, I want you to notice the heft or weight of it. Allow your thoughts to focus on the look and shape of that pebble, its edges and curves, crevasses. Notice its temperature, whether it is comfortably warm, or cool as it nestles into the palm of your hand.

And then use your imagination to make the pebble heavier and heavier—larger and larger—and heavier. So heavy it is becoming a burden, so heavy it is almost impossible to hold up. And then in an instant notice that you can make it lighter and lighter, smaller and smaller, so small *it is shrinking away, shrinking away to the size of a single grain of sand becoming lost in the whorls and vastness of the palm of your hand. So small, so light, so inconsequential that you realize you could easily, effortlessly, shrink it away to nothing, as if it had never been.*

And as you toss that bit of sand aside, inconsequential, walking along comfortably, in the cool of the green-dappled shade, you can hear in the distance the sound of a waterfall. As you continue to go deeper into the forest, the surge of the waterfall sounds louder and louder, until you come around a bend and there it is right before you.

You can feel the cool of the spray, comfortable, and hear the giant roar of the cascading water, so loud. But part of you knows that this is your place, your space. You are in control here, deep in your own mind. And I wonder if your imagination is powerful enough to turn down that roaring, cascading sound. Almost as if you have a remote control in your hand, turning down the volume, quieter and quieter, until there is blessed silence.

Without warning the loud powerful roar comes back, but in an instant your finger has found the mute button on your control, and everything is calm—quiet. Amazing how powerful you imagination is.

Now as you are so relaxed and comfortable, focusing on the sound of my voice, it may be there is a place in your body where you have felt discomfort. Now I don't know if that place will feel a little better now if it is a little warmer – or cooler. Or if it will feel so much better if you simply breathe deeply and allow the healthy muscles surrounding that part of your body to relax now.

But I wonder, if that discomfort of the past was a color, I wonder what color would it be? I wonder if your imagination is powerful enough to imagine that color. I wonder if you can imagine that color within your body, almost as though you could look into your body, so you could see that color filling the area where that old discomfort of the past used to be.

Now of course there is another color, a different color, a color of health and healing, of peace. And I don't know what that healthy, comfortable, peaceful color is. But part of you knows. I wonder if your other-than-conscious is powerful enough to richly, vividly imagine that color of comfort and health. And as you imagine it, I wonder if you can imagine that color changing shade by shade, hue by hue from that old uncomfortable color of the past, to this new, beautiful color of comfort. I wonder if you can see that new color of comfort filling that part of your body, everywhere that old color used to be.

And as you realize that that old discomfort of the past used to have a heft or weight to it, it wonder if your powerful other-than-conscious mind is powerful enough to imagine it shrinking away, away, further and further away; letting it go, shrinking so small, inconsequential, like a grain of sand, becoming lost among all the healthy tissues of the body— and finally disappearing as the tissues of the body return to their natural, normal, healthy texture and color.

And of course this is what your body actually does best, heal itself at the phenomenal rate of 50 million cells a second, changing and rearranging in the right sequence and the right order for you. Creating health, harmony, and vitality in your body.

And it may be that that old discomfort of the past used to have a sound to it, maybe even a roar—but now notice that you have control! You may not even notice how remote that old sensation is becoming as it just fades away. And if it had a roar, I wonder if you can use that volume control to just fade it away, quieter and quieter, until—everything is at peace. Peace. Comfort. You notice just how good your body feels, now.

Your body and your powerful other-than-conscious mind will continue to create this peace and this healing.

As you notice how good, how relaxed and comfortable you feel, you find that if this is a time to sleep, you can just let yourself slip into a deep dreamy sleep now. This is the time when your body is healing, rejuvenating. Your mind is at peace. You are sleeping so deeply, so comfortably through the night. Sleeping so deeply, so comfortably that outside sounds and influences, as long as they are safe, only carry you deeper, giving you beautiful dreams of your future—filled with health and harmony and happiness.

Of course if this is a time to be awake and conscious, you can begin the process of coming back into the room. When you are ready to feel good for no apparent reason at all, when you feel comfortable and ready to enjoy the rest of your day—then at that moment your eyes will open! You will be wide awake, feeling great and realizing, of course, that every day in every way, your life is getting better, your world is getting better, and this is so.

Script: Direct Suggestions for Numbness

Glove anesthesia is handy traditional way to deal with pain. Many people experience numbness simply as part of the hypnotic process, without any suggestions for anesthesia. This takes advantage of the natural numbness or anesthesia which occurs at level three or four hypnotic depth on Aron's depth scale. This is my version. Any induction is fine.

By the way, I would *not* use this process if the person is actually experiencing pain in her or his hands! Remember, you want to shift focus away from the area of discomfort, not confront it directly.

As you go deeper, deeper now, you notice that your hands are becoming comfortably, completely totally numb, so comfortably completely totally numb. It does not matter how you do this, or how your other-than-conscious simply does it for you. The only thing which is important is that you understand that you can lose sensations as easily as turning off a light, closing a door.

As you sleep so deeply you don't even notice when your body fades away, as it always does, allowing you to sleep so deeply, so comfortably. And I don't know where you will begin to experience that numb feeling first. Perhaps on the back of the left hand, or the numb thumb of the right hand, whatever is right for you right now, as all sensation has left that hand right now. But a part of you knows, and I wonder if you can reach over to that numb hand and begin to touch it. You might feel that sensation at first, but soon it simply fades away, gone from your thoughts, gone from your mind, gone from your body's awareness. As you begin to pinch yourself, a feeling you may feel at first, so you realize that it simply fades away, gone, as your hands drift back to their resting position.

Isn't it comforting to realize your body can create this numb comfort any time it is useful for you? That your body creates this fade every night? It is as natural as sleeping.

Now there may have been some part of your body which used to feel discomfort. You might find that your numb hand just drifts there now, to touch that part of your body which used to feel discomfort—and as it does an amazing thing happens, that numbness just flows, creating that comfortable numb sensation wherever you touch.

Or it may be that your hand simply rests, comfortably numb, as a part of you realizes that you can create that numbness anywhere you like, any time you like. In fact you probably don't even realize how much better you feel, now.

From here you can transition into any emerging, or continue with another aspect of the hypnotic process.

Script: Remote Control Metaphor
Any induction is fine!

Everyone credits Marconi with inventing the radio, but sometimes we don't even realize the power we have. That was true with Nikola Tesla, who worked with radio waves years before. But if Marconi played the mamba so we listen to the radio, Tesla was just interested in turning off a light.

We take it for granted now, how easy it is to make a change. You change channels on your TV with your remote control, and you don't even think about it. There was even that device a few years ago where you could walk into a room and simply clap—and the lights would turn on or off. And now some people even have apps on their phones to turn on the air conditioning and make their home so much more comfortable—from so far away.

It is amazing really, like magic, having that kind of control from a distance, that sort of power. And that's what Tesla wanted, to send a remote signal, and simply turn off the light. Radio waves. We take it for granted, really, but imagine how magical that seemed, with the flick of a button, a light across the room simply turns off.

When was the last time you looked at the fuse box in your home? It has probably been a while. It is something you don't even think about. All those circuits, switches, circuit breakers. Behind the box there are wires running through all those switches, carrying the power from one place to another, all going through those switches.

Have you considered that the body is like that? The nerves of the body carry signals from each part of the body to the brain. If you could look at it there would be a switch for the feeling in the hands, the calves, the toes, the head, the shoulders, and every other part of the body [you can include the part which has been hurting in this list, somewhere in the middle of the list, but move past it quickly—do not emphasize it].

What would it be like if you could simply throw a switch, and then no sensation could get through there, no sensation at all? How much better would you feel?

But think about it, really; why even go to the fuse box, when you can just have that control, right there. Imagine the possibility of just holding that remote, turning the dials of comfort and discomfort, and adjusting things to just the right level for you. How good would it feel if you could create the perfect level of comfort for yourself right now?

Because Tesla knew that was power, just being able to turn something off, across the room. Just like magic. But right now it is probably just better to remember old Marconi and his magic music box, to focus on the music playing, going deeper now, the music simply carrying you deeper, feeling fine, feeling at peace...

You can go to a deepener and then another part of the process, or any emerging. If emerging, emphasize how comfortable the client feels as he or she comes back into the room.

Hands and Feet: a Quick Metaphor

Remember, if pain is in the core of the body or the head it is often more intense that if it is in the arms or legs. For this reason it can be useful to move the pain outward, and then out of the body. Another idea here is to focus on the hands or feet feeling good as a distraction from other body discomfort.

It is not a good idea to move pain into the body from the arms or legs! Nor would you focus on the hands or feet if the client is experiencing pain in the hands or feet. Remember, you always deemphasize the part of the body which has been uncomfortable.

These brief metaphors are not long enough to stand as full processes, but you could use them within a longer process or even as part of the emerging:

...And as you feel so good now, you can just let that old discomfort go, just let it flow. Let it flow to the hands and feet, then imagine the possibility of the hands and feet actually opening up, releasing, letting go, and just let that old discomfort flow away, away, further and further away.

...And as you notice how comfortable you feel now, I want you to notice just how good your hands and feet feel. As you come back into the room you feel so comfortable and you notice your hands and feet feel so very good. Wide awake, now!

As the client emerges back into the room, say *You feel good! How do you feel? And your back* [or whatever part of the body which was in pain] *feels good? And your hands and feet feel good! It is probably a good idea now for you to focus on just how good your hands and feet feel, now.*

9 FEARS

Carla looked at me, her features drawn. In her late thirties, she looked fit but very tense.

"I'm afraid of horses."

"Okay," I said, "Tell me a little more. Are you around horses a lot?"

"I'm an equestrian. I own horses, I train horses. Horses are my life." Now she looked really scared. I could see tears of frustration beginning to well up in her eyes.

I had seen this sort of thing before, in other clients: The pilot who developed a fear of flying; the truck driver who panicked at the thought of getting on the Interstate. These were fears which were especially distressing and debilitating because they struck not only at the person's livelihood, but also at their most basic self-identity and self-concept.

There have been many other clients with fears over the years—of water, driving, driving over bridges, bugs, snakes, lizards, airports, public speaking, test anxiety, leaving the house, and so on.

One of the most memorable was the woman who panicked when she got too hot—a real problem since she lives in South Carolina where the summers can be sweltering. Another was a woman who was afraid of the rain, and had to actually check the weather forecast before she would schedule an appointment with me.

The consequences of these fears can be dramatic. In South Carolina, a fear of the rain or heat can essentially lead to self-imprisonment at home. I have had clients who lost their jobs because of fears. Test anxiety can prevent a person from getting a professional license and moving ahead with his or her career.

Sometimes fear responses build gradually, over time, or perhaps they have "always" been around. In the case of the pilot, the fear crept up gradually. The truck driver suddenly realized one day that he was sweating profusely and squeezing the steering wheel with a vice-like grip.

"Tell me a little more," I asked Carla.

"I was riding Hank—he's big, like a Clydesdale, 15 hands. And he's a great horse, very calm. We were with another horse, a new one I'm training, and she spooked. And he spooked and threw me. It was so fast, unexpected, and I hit the ground so hard. It knocked me out for a few seconds. I didn't break anything, but I really bruised my hip and leg—I couldn't get up at first. I know how to ride and I know how to fall, but since then it's getting harder and harder to climb back into the saddle. I'm afraid."

She was intense as she spoke. I could see the strain in her face.

Typically, irrational fears are easy to address with hypnosis. Fears which have been present for a long time and are part of a person's ego integrity or self-identity can be more difficult to address, but in her case it seemed like a recent phenomenon. The fact that it touched on her livelihood made it more difficult, since Carla was focusing a lot of emotional energy into it, but I was still confident we would succeed—and we did.

Pre-talk Considerations for Fears and Panic

The pre-talk before working on an irrational fear, phobia, or panic attacks can be fairly brief. The approach I take is solution-focused: where are you now, where do you want to be—let's move from here to there. Generally I am not interested in the "cause" of the problem; focusing on a problem or a supposed cause tends to emotionally reinforce it as a problem. Even though Carla pointed to a specific situation as a root of her fear, most of the time clients do not have any specific incident in mind as a genesis.

It is helpful to have a brief description of the circumstances which lead to the fear response. You want to know what triggers the fear in the client. There are some key questions I always ask:

Let's say we take care of this problem. How will your life be better?

It is important to know a client's positive motivation, and what she or he thinks of as success. Write down his or her exact words (like bullet points—you are after key phrases, not paragraphs).

When you're in that situation, how do you feel?

Again, jot down key phrases. After the initial answer you will also want to ask, *how do you feel physically?* and *how do you feel emotionally?* Try not to suggest any feelings or sensations. You might say something like, *Most people feel this sort of thing in their body—what sensations do you have?*

Typical physical answers include rapid heartbeat, shallow or trouble breathing, sweaty palms, dry mouth, and so on. On the emotional side, often clients will say things like "panicked," "frightened," "I can't think," "nervous," or "my mind goes blank." Again, try not to suggest anything, or if you absolutely must give an example, quickly and briefly provide three or four. You are interested in the client's own terminology and conception of the problem.

Script: Theater of the Mind: A Quick Release for Fear

Once you are done with the pre-talk and have the answers to the questions above, you are ready for the hypnosis process. You can use any induction to begin. I like to use a progressive relaxation with ego strengtheners for this, since it is about creating a soothing body experience and emotional strength. Also, it is important to create the theater in the metaphor as a safe place. You are dealing with fear; the client needs a safe haven. After the induction, move into the hypnosis process:

I'd like to invite you to imagine that you are walking down a set of steps deep inside your own mind. I don't know whether these steps are enclosed and comfortable or open and airy and beautiful, but a part of you knows, and whatever you are experiencing it is appropriate for you. With each step you go down, you feel more comfortable and relaxed, feeling deep sensations of relaxation moving through your body now. With each step down you feel safer and more secure—after all this is your mind. One at a time, down those steps. More relaxed, more secure. Stepping down, down, down...

Until you come to this room at the bottom. As you enter the room you realize this is a movie theater, your own personal movie theater in your mind. As you enter this room, you realize that you are completely safe, totally comfortable, absolutely at ease in this, your theater. Enjoying the room, you realize there is but one chair in this room; after all, this is your theater. As you allow yourself to rest down into the chair now, you notice that it is a thousand times more comfortable than the surface you are resting on here in my office. Notice how the chair supports you, beneath your head, beneath your arms, behind your shoulders—in the same way your powerful other-than-conscious always supports you, causing your heart to beat rhythmically, naturally, normally over 86 thousand times a day.

As you rest comfortably into the chair, your eye gently drifts up to the movie screen, and you notice that a movie is playing. It is a movie of your life. In this movie you can see yourself [describe client entering into the situation in which he or she felt panic; (e.g., walking up to the front of the room to give a speech, going into the classroom to take a test, walking onto an airplane, etc.].

As you watch this movie, you realize you are completely safe here, comfortable in the movie theater, and comfortable in my office. On the screen you can see how uncomfortable you look as you [walk into the plane, etc.]

You can see it on your face, you know that [describe the client's negative emotional and physical feelings/experiences in the situation, using his or her own words as much as possible. For invisible experiences, you can say things like, As you watch this you just know that, there on the screen, your heart is racing OR you know your mind is a blank, etc.]

But as you watch this movie, notice that an interesting thing is happening, notice that all the colors in the picture are just fading away, fading to sepia tones, to pastels. Fading to black and white. As the colors fade away notice that the sounds of this place [if there are specific sounds associated with this place, such as sound from a crowd, or the air rushing over the plane, or voices, etc., mention them]. *The sounds are simply fading away, growing quieter and quieter, like someone turning down a volume control. Quieter and quieter and quieter—until they are completely silent. And as the color and the sound fades away, notice that all the motion in this picture is grinding to a halt. Everything is slowing down, until it completely stops.*

And you realize you are not looking at a movie at all. You are just looking at a picture, like a photograph, like an old black and white snapshot. It is a part of your past, a part of who you used to be, but it has nothing to do with your present, and certainly nothing to do with your future.

Reach up and take it down off the wall. Put a frame around it. Make the frame old and dingy, like you might find at a garage sale, something you no longer want or need or even care about. And just take it back behind you, two to 300 feet behind you, and just let it go. Let it go. Put it away. It is a part of your past, a part of who you used to be, but it has nothing to do with your present, and certainly nothing to do with your future. And as you release and you allow and you let it go, feel the healing take place!

As you turn back to your chair, it is gone from your thoughts, gone from your mind, gone from your body's awareness. So easy to remember to forget by simply forgetting to remember.

As you return to your chair, settling into the chair, realizing how it supports you, beneath your head, beneath your arms, behind your shoulders, you realize that you are not just the audience for this movie. You are in fact the producer, the director. This is, after all, a movie of your life. And as your eyes drift up to the screen, you notice that the same movie is playing again. It is the same thing only different.

You see yourself [describe client entering the situation that] in the past [caused the panic], *but as you look at your face, you realize* [describe the positive opposite of the client's previous physical and emotional reaction; e.g., your face shows a calm confidence, your heartbeat is deep and rhythmic and steady, your breathing is deep and from the diaphragm, you mouth is moist, your hands are steady, your feet are solid beneath you, your powerful mind/memory serves you well, your words/thoughts flow easily, fluidly, comfortably, etc.; use the client's own language as much as possible].

Notice that the colors are becoming more vivid and bright. Notice that the sounds are crisp and clear. Notice that the motion is fluid and comfortable. And just take a moment to enjoy this wonderful movie, and when my voice returns, it will only prompt you to enter an even deeper level of relaxation now.

[Pause perhaps 20 seconds—less if you do not have music]

Deeper now! More relaxed than ever before. Drifting, floating, dreaming, flowing. So comfortable, going even deeper now. You are watching a different movie, so comfortable in your theater. In this movie [very briefly describe another incident in which the client previously felt panicked, with a very brief description of the associated physical and emotional feelings, using the client's own terms], *but notice that the colors are already fading away, fading to black and white. The sounds are already becoming silent. The motion is already stopping. And you realize that you are not looking at a movie at all —this is just a picture, like an old black and white snapshot. Something perhaps tattered and yellowed. It is a part of your past, a part of who you used to be, but it has nothing to do with your present, and certainly nothing to do with your future.*

Reach up and take it down off the wall. Put a frame around it. Make the frame old, like you might see at a museum, something representing the ancient past. Take it back two to 300 feet behind you, and just let it go. Let it go. Put it away. It is a part of your past, a part of who you used to be, but it has nothing to do with your present, and certainly nothing to do with your future. And as you release and you allow and you let it go, feel the healing take place!

As you turn back to your chair, it is gone from your thoughts, gone from your mind, gone from your body's awareness.

Setting into your chair, so relaxed and so comfortable, you can see your movie playing again. [Briefly describe the same scene, but this time the client sees himself or herself experiencing positive sensations and feelings in the situation. Use the client's language as much as possible]. *Notice that the colors are bright and vivid, the sounds are crisp and clear, the motion is fluid. And you realize you are okay. You are absolutely all right. So just take a moment to enjoy this movie, and when my voice returns, I wonder just how much more deeply you can relax now.*

[Pause perhaps 10 seconds].

Emerging: *Deeper now! So relaxed and so comfortable! In a moment it will be time to return back into this place, back into this room. As you come back into the room, notice just how good, just how comfortable you feel. You feel energized and renewed, looking forward to a great rest of the day! When you are ready to feel good for no apparent reason, then your eyes will open. You will be wide awake! Wide awake! Feeling fine and in perfect health. Realizing that every day, in every way, your life is getting better, your world is getting better, and this is so!*

Awake: *You feel good! How do you feel?*

Script: The Three Doors: A Process for Seeing Options

The Three Doors is a great follow up for a second session in addressing fears. However, this process is really about seeing options. People tend to get emotionally stuck and follow patterns, without realizing that at any one moment in time they have a number of options. This process is excellent for any recurring situation which leads to stress, frustration or emotional discomfort. Any induction will do to begin. Then say:

As you are going deeper now, I wonder how relaxed and comfortable you can become. So as you continue to relax now, I wonder if you can imagine that you are walking down a series of steps deep into your own mind, one at a time, down those steps. With each step you go deeper, with each step safer and more comfortable. Now I don't know if the stairway is wide open and spacious and beautiful, or if it is enclosed and secure and comfortable, but your powerful other-than-conscious mind knows exactly what is right for you now.

Going deeper and deeper, step by step, safer and more secure.

Until you come to this room, with three doors. In this room with three doors you are absolutely safe, totally comfortable, completely at peace. At any one moment in time there is only an infinity of choices you can make, and this room is your place to see those choices, to make the changes you want to make.

So I would like to invite you to think of a situation which, in the past, has made you anxious or frustrated or uncomfortable. Step into it, feel it, hear it—hear what is being said, if anything is being said, or any other sounds, or smells.

And now notice the three doors. Each door represents the possibility of change. When you step through a door you will be in that place, at that time, living that experience.

But this time, something new is happening. You are handling that old situation in a way that is so creative, so powerful, so much more positive, so much better than you did in the past. It does not matter if you don't know, right now, how to handle things differently. That powerful, other-than-conscious, creative part of you knows. No matter what happens around you, you own your own responses! At each moment there is an infinity of choices you can make.

So take a deep breath, let it out slowly, and step through the first door. As you step through the door, notice that that old situation which used to frustrate you is happening again.

But this time you are handling it differently, in a way that is so positive, so productive, so beneficial that you are surprising even yourself. Just let that scene play out now. And when my voice returns you will go even deeper.

[Pause 10 to 20 seconds—less if you do not have music.]

Deeper now, more relaxed than ever before, drifting, dreaming, floating, flowing. Here in the room with three doors you are absolutely safe, totally comfortable, completely at peace. This is your opportunity to dream and to create change!

So let your eye drift to the second door. As you step through the second door, that same old situation will be playing out—but this time you are not reacting like you did in the past, and you are not even responding in the great way you did behind the first door, as positive as that was. No, now you are responding in a new, different, wonderful way which is so positive and so productive that you are surprising even yourself! So just step through the second door, and let it happen now.

[Pause 10 to 20 seconds.]

Deeper now! Here in the room with three doors you are absolutely safe, totally comfortable, completely at peace. This is your opportunity to see things differently, through new eyes, from better and healthier perspectives. This is your opportunity to do things differently, to make choices.

So notice the third door. [As you do this part, giggle.]

The same old thing is gonna happen again behind the third door—you sure won't handle it in the tired old way you did in the past, or even the great ways you did behind the first two doors. Nope! This time you're going to handle it in a way that is so silly, so ridiculous, that you might not even do this in real life. Just have a good time and enjoy it! Step through the door now!

[Pause 10 to 20 seconds.]

[Not giggling]: *Here in the room with three doors you are absolutely safe, totally comfortable, completely at peace. You can come here any time, to make changes, to see things in new ways, to respond to life positively and differently.*

Now when you are ready to see through new eyes, in different ways, from better and healthier perspectives, your eyes will open. As your eyes open, you feel wide awake, refreshed, fine and in perfect health! Wide awake! You feel great!

You feel great! How do you feel?

10 REGRESSION: DEALING WITH TRAUMA

"As you look up and down the hallway, you realize that there is a door which you need to go through today. Even if you don't know which one, a part of you knows what is right for you, which will help you. Go ahead and step through the door." I am leading a client through a process of regression. She is clearly relaxed and under.

"It's so bad, it's so bad! He's spent all that money." Immediately she starts sobbing.

"Where are you?"

"In our house. In the kitchen."

"How old are you?"

Shakes her head. "I don't...26."

"What's happening?" I ask.

"He's just told me about all that money he spent. We're fighting."

"There's an emotion you feel right now, a negative, less-than-positive emotion. It does not matter if you can't name it; part of you knows what it is. Where do you feel it in your body?"

Still, crying her hand moves to her chest. "All through here."

"I'd like you to imagine that that emotion has a color. What color is it?"

"Deep, deep purple..."

The Basic Idea

Past traumatic or problematic events can result in an emotional fixation in which current events or circumstances can trigger an intrusion of those emotions from the past, bringing them into the present. These re-experienced emotions can be very traumatic, or at least troubling, when they intrude into the present.

Regression is a hypnotic process for resetting past emotions. It can be very powerful and freeing. The approach is useful in addressing a variety of problems.

Remember that only a qualified mental health or medical professional should treat anxiety disorders, including post-traumatic stress disorder (PTSD) and mood disorders. If you are a lay hypnotist and your client is presenting problems which seem to be above your level of training or experience, refer the client to a qualified professional.

Even if you think you know your client's history, you may be surprised at what the client will open when she or he steps through that door. At times in my practice we have stepped into the middle of a rape that the client had not disclosed in advance.

For example, there was this experience:

"Where are you now?" I asked.

"I'm in the emergency room—they called and told me to come quickly, that my husband was injured at work." She is under, but her face is tense, drawn.

"What's happening?"

"I'm at the desk, asking the nurse where Sam is. The doctor is there—he says 'Oh, didn't you know, he's dead?' And oh my god, he's just told me that he's dead. My husband is dead!" She's sobbing now, almost screaming.

"There is with you an Older, Wiser You," I say. "She can do anything she needs to do to help you, take any action, say anything, meld with you, whatever she needs to do to help you."

Typically Older Wiser Yous offer comfort, like a hug.

"What's she doing now?" I ask.

"She's jumped on the doctor and she is biting him!"

"Okay," I say.

"Now she is screaming and beating him with her fists." The client breaks down in sobs; she is still under.

Regression is not for the timid, or for novice hypnotists. You need to be experienced and familiar with hypnotic processes and language before you do this. Remember, your first goal is the safety of your client.

Also, as I use it, regression is not problem-focused. Regression techniques are solution-focused. The goal is not to provide insight into past problems, but rather to create the possibility of powerful emotional change in the present and future.

Introducing the Concept to the Client

I never do the regression during the same session in which I introduce the concept. This is a significant emotional process, and I want the client to have time to engage with it. Also, it is critical that our professional relationship of rapport and trust is firmly established. The following is not a hypnosis script, but it is how I explain regression to a client:

Would you agree that you have more wisdom, life experience, emotional strength now than you did in the past?

That is sort of a truism, but I want you thinking about it. So you had experiences in the past which may have been problematic or traumatic. You handled them as well as you could at the time, but if you had it to do over, would you do it differently?

So there were emotions associated with those events, and sometimes things today can trigger those emotions, but they don't belong here. They are not today's emotions. The problems of the past are being imported into the present.

The purpose of regression is to go back into the past, to re-live the troubling event, to allow you to re-handle it using today's emotional strength and resources.

Most people who experience this process feel sort of emotionally flat for a short time—perhaps even an hour or two afterward. If you think about it, that makes sense. But it is not a problem; you will be fine in a short time. The process tends to be very healing.

Sometimes I will use the metaphor of cleaning infection out of the body as an analogy to regression. Once all of this has been discussed with the client, we can move forward at the next session.

The Basic Pattern
There is no set method or script for regression. This is an interactive process, meaning that the client will be talking and interacting while in the hypnotic state. Remember, it is very important to establish an emotional safe place when you undertake this process. Notice that I use the metaphor of a hallway with many doors for this safe place. The client will be talking, so you cannot predict what she or he will say.

Begin with any hypnotic induction. I like to use progressive relaxation with ego strengtheners, or a confusion induction. As you finish the induction, move to a deepener—like the stairwell:

As you feel so relaxed, so comfortable and safe now, I wonder what it would be like if you could double or triple that level of relaxation. Imagine walking down a stairwell deep into your own mind. With each step you go deeper. With each step more relaxed, with each step safer and more secure. Each word takes you deeper, each step takes you deeper. There is a part of you which has always known that you can speak to me in a hypnotic state, that each word you say takes you even deeper, until the very words themselves can become unconscious, automatic. Deeper and deeper, step by step, safer and more secure.

[Establish a metaphor for the regression. Establish this as a safe place.]

As you reach the bottom of the stairs you step into a long hallway with many doors. In this hallway with many doors you are absolutely safe, totally comfortable, completely at peace. You can return to this hallway at any time.

As you look at the doors—and it does not matter if you see them or just pretend them, or experience them in some other way—there is a part of you that realizes that each doorway represents a portal, an entryway into the past.

When you step through the doorway you will be in that place, at that time, living that experience. There is a part of you which knows what door to go through now, which will help you. Just step up to the door, and when you are ready, step through now.

Be there in that moment. Breathe it in, feel it, be there in that moment. Hear what is being said, if anything is said, and any other sounds, or smells.

Where are you?

How old are you?

What is happening?

At this point scripting becomes difficult. A key metaphor to use is the Older Wiser You.

After the person has engaged the experience:

There is with you now an older, wiser you. S/he has more wisdom, life experience, and emotional strength. S/he can do whatever s/he needs to do to help you. S/he can say anything, take any action, meld with you, comfort you— whatever you need. What is s/he doing now?

Begin to work through the issues raised. Remember, the goal is not to gain insight or to find supposed "causes." The experience may or may not be a memory. The client has engaged an emotional metaphor to help her or him address the current problem. Stay focused on reframing the narrative in a positive way, in moving past it. Rather than giving advice, ask what the older wiser you is saying or doing. The person has the resources to create a solution. The goal is not to advise the client, but to engage the client in solution thinking.

Another useful technique is the crystal vial. When the client is experiencing strong emotion, this can be a very helpful metaphor. I like the archaic term "vial" because it is a homophone for vile—something disgusting and bad. Also, a vial takes a "stopper" rather than just a lid. The purpose of the vial is to get rid of something bad.

Right now, you feel a strong negative emotion in your body. It does not matter if you can't name it; part of you knows what it is. What parts of your body is that negative emotion touching? Where do you feel it in your body?

If that negative, less-than-positive emotion was a color, I wonder what color it would be. Imagine that that negative, less-than-positive color was touching your body, everywhere that old negative emotion was. You might even imagine that your body is like crystal, so you can see that old, negative color of the past.

Now I'd like to invite you to imagine that you have, in your hand, a crystal vial, like a jar. And begin to imagine that all that old negative, less-than-positive color is flowing out into that vial. That jar, that vial can hold every bit of it. Just let it all go, let it all flow. As that negative, less-than-positive emotion flows out of your body, just let it go. Feel the healing take place. Let it all go. Is it all gone?

Would you like to put a stopper in it, put a cap on it? Do it! Now what would you like to do with that vial?

Put the vial away. Sometimes the client wants to throw it away, bury it, cast it into the sea, give it to the Older Wiser You, or give it to Jesus. Tell her or him to do it, to let it go, and feel the healing taking place. Then:

Now there is another emotion. A strong, powerful emotion, which is the opposite of that old negative emotion of the past. It does not matter if you cannot name that strong, positive emotion. There is a part of you which knows exactly what that emotion is, what it feels like. If that strong, positive emotion was a color, what color would it be?

Imagine that that new color, that strong positive color fills the environment around you. Imagine that you could breathe it in deeply, into your body. As you breathe it in, feel it filling your body—first wherever you felt that old, negative emotion of the past, and then flowing throughout your body. Feel this new, strong, positive emotion!

At some point you may want to ask the client if there is anything else she or he needs to do here in this place. If so, do it. When the client is ready, step back into the hallway with many doors (reinforcing that here in the hallway with many doors you are absolutely safe, totally comfortable, completely at peace).

Do not be afraid to address strong emotion; that is the purpose of this process. However, remember that you can pull the client back into the hallway with many doors at any time if this will help. The Older Wiser You can also come into the hallway to interact with the client. The crystal vial process can also take place in the hallway.

Often you will want to ask if there is another doorway which you need to visit today. Sometimes a regression may involve visiting two or three doors.

The client may change the hallway into some other metaphor. That's okay—go with it. This process is very fluid and flexible. Just remember to maintain a safe place. Remember to keep your focus on solutions.

One day a client told me, "It's not a hallway."

"Oh," I said, "Where are we?"

"It is beautiful here—with white marble, and Greek columns, all around us in a circle. It's a temple."

"You're absolutely safe, totally comfortable here in the temple," I said.

"There's a problem though—that pit."

"Tell me about the pit." I said.

"Right in the center. It is awful, dark, it feels terrible."

"Okay," I say. "What needs to happen with the pit?"

"I'm going to make it a swimming pool, with crystal blue water. And water lilies."

It was a great example of a healing, emotional reframe, created completely by the client.

Use Ericksonian inferred language patterns and agreement with a twist (as in motivational interviewing), rather than direct advice, to reframe the client's narrative into a solution narrative.

At the end, you might invite the client to select a door where a positive, strong memory occurred. He or she can step through the door, and take as much time as she or he likes enjoying that experience. The seconds are like minutes here, and the hours are like days. Pause for perhaps 10 or 15 seconds while the client enjoys this experience.

Another regression metaphor is the affect bridge. This involves visualizing the first time the negative emotion was experienced, and then asking the client to visualize some sort of physical connection between the client now and that event (the client normally describes something like a rope, chain, thread, string, beam of light, beam of darkness, etc.). Then ask the client how to cut or break that connection.

She or he will tell you how to do that (cut it with scissors, use an axe, the Older Wiser You cuts it, etc.), and then just tell the client to have that happen. Reinforce new feelings, and stronger, future-oriented emotions.

Conclude with a standard emerging.

Remember, the client may be a little washed out or flat after the emotional intensity of the regression. Reinforce things positively. Assure him or her that she will feel better soon, and that this is a path to healing.

Memory, Past Lives, & Causes

Remember that hypnosis is about emotional change, not truth. There is no guarantee that even "this life" experiences actually happened. We know that memory is powerfully framed by emotion, and is malleable or changeable over time. Use caution as you use regression processes; remember that by creating experience, you can inadvertently create trauma. The goal, of course, is to do the opposite.

Many people are curious about past lives, and past life regression. I tend to see reports of past lives as simply another hypnotic metaphor, an emotional way of handling a current problem. I reframe these "memories" in the same way. You might consider engaging a "higher you" to assist the client rather than an Older Wiser You.

Remember, just because a client "recalls" an "event" in a regression session, this does not mean that the event "caused" the current problem. Emotions are fundamentally non-rational, and notions of causality are probably not helpful. If the client sees the event as the cause, then it becomes the cause, and should be addressed as such (even if objectively this is not the cause, or there were many other plausible or contributing causes). Remember, the "event" may not even be objectively real. The reality of the emotional metaphor is not important for healing.

Carl Sagan (1996) documents an interesting fringe example of false memory creating. He notes that therapists who specialize in UFO abductions and those who specialize in Satanic ritual abuse each find high incidences of these traumas in their client populations—to the point where a reasonable extrapolation would be that these are widespread, significant social problems. However, UFO specialists don't tend to find anyone abused by Satanists, and vice versa. Clearly the therapist's expectation is framing the client's perception.

Also, remember that clients can be traumatized by framing metaphors or events as traumas. As evidence, see examples of child sexual abuse hysteria, including the Kern County cases, Little Rascals day care case, and the McMartin day care case (there are many similar). In each of these cases, events were described by children, under the leading of therapists, which were so over the top they simply could not have occurred. Although these cases led to convictions, many were overturned or pardons were granted because of the absurd nature of the testimony. One huge tragedy, though, was that these children were traumatized through the intervention of incompetent therapists. The goal is to help the client release the past and move forward. The goal is for the client to become not-a-victim, in the sense that she or he has moved past the experience, learned from it, and grown.

11 PATTERNS OF HYPNOTIC LANGAUGE

This book has presented a number of scripts. These are useful for developing the skill of hypnosis and learning patterns of hypnotic language; however, mastery of hypnosis must involve developing the ability to create your own hypnotic processes. Often this is done extemporaneously in the session as you create a process to address the unique concerns the client has raised.

It is always necessary to read a script and make it your own, by modifying the language to be more comfortable for your pattern of speaking. There is a bigger idea here, though. The stories and metaphors in any script are by someone else. As a hypnotist, it is important to develop the skill of using your own experience and stories to create processes of change for clients. Milton Erickson was a genius, but it would be a mistake to simply try to use his stories to create change. Jennings and Skovholt (1999) in their article, "The cognitive, emotional, and relational characteristics of master therapists," note that master therapists draw upon their own rich life and work experiences in their work. This does not mean that therapists make the counseling session about themselves; rather, their own stories help them help clients rework their stories.

In addition to explicit stories and metaphors, patterns of language can be helpful in creating and managing suggestions. Developing the skill of suggestion management, the ability to use emotional language to help clients create change, is the goal of the master hypnotist.

These language patterns can be used in both the relaxed Theta state as well as with clients in a waking state— Erickson's "ordinary waking state" work, or when working with awake clients using a Motivational Interviewing approach. Here are several basic language patterns and techniques.

Truisms & Clichés

Truisms are basic statements of fact which are essentially unarguable.

- There's no place like home.
- A mind is a terrible thing to waste.
- A penny saved is a penny earned.
- It is important to get a good education.
- All roads lead to Rome.
- Beauty is in the eye of the beholder.
- She thought she could do it. So she did.
- The life you save may be your own.

Brief sayings or phrases attributed to fortune cookies, bumper stickers, Benjamin Franklin, Confucius, Shakespeare, or the Bible's book of Proverbs can often fit this category. These can even be catchphrases or Internet memes which appear for a moment in the pop culture. Essentially these simple statements would be used as a springboard to more complex concepts as the session goes on.

Forer Effect or Barnum Statements

Forer effect statements are personality descriptions supposedly tailored specifically for an individual, but which are actually vague general statements which could apply to anyone. These are also called Barnum Statements after the famous showman P. T. Barnum who used this to amaze, befuddle and rip off his patrons. Horoscopes make their living off Forer effect statements.

Bertram Forer's original "analysis" given to participants in his study perfectly illustrates this type of statement:

You have a great need for other people to like and admire you. You have a tendency to be critical of yourself. You have a great deal of unused capacity which you have not turned to your advantage. While you have some personality weaknesses, you are generally able to compensate for them. Your sexual adjustment has presented problems for you. Disciplined and self-controlled outside, you tend to be worrisome and insecure inside. At times you have serious doubts as to whether you have made the right decision or done the right thing. You prefer a certain amount of change and variety and become dissatisfied when hemmed in by restrictions and limitations. You pride yourself as an independent thinker and do not accept others' statements without satisfactory proof. You have found it unwise to be too frank in revealing yourself to others. At times you are extroverted, affable, sociable, while at other times you are introverted, wary, reserved. Some of your aspirations tend to be pretty unrealistic. Security is one of your major goals in life. (1949)

Essentially, Forer effect statements are truisms. This sort of statement would be used to introduce a vague concept which would then be developed as the session progresses.

Vague Possibilities

Truisms and Forer effect statements are true but trite. They do not really mean anything; they simply introduce concepts. Vague, open statements go a step further and are designed to get the client thinking about other possibilities:

- There are a lot of ways to get an education.
- You probably already know many ways to handle stress.
- There are a lot of ways to get from here to Albuquerque.
- You could look at it that way, if you wanted to.
- What if you wanted to take a different road?

The goal here is to help the client begin to move from stuck thinking to unstuck thinking. At any one moment in time there are only an infinity of possibilities. Even though we can fall into seeing by looking through blinders—and seeing only one or a few options—in reality, there are always many options and possibilities.

Creating Experience
Creating experience is inviting the client to enter into an emotional experience in the session. The goal will then be to use the emotion generated to help create a change. Examples of creating experience would be:

- Think about how luxurious it feels when you let a DoveBar melt in your mouth.
- You know what it is like to have one of those perfect conversations, with the right guy, where everything just seems to click? And you can really feel the connection?
- You know what it feels like when you've really overeaten and you feel so...yech. Now think about how good you feel when you eat just the right amount for you.
- You know what it feels like after a workout when you're getting cleaned up and you feel physically good!
- I wonder just how good you would feel after a good night's sleep!

Hidden Commands
Reactance is a normal response when you tell someone what to do—the person tends to resist and not want to follow your instructions. This is why giving advice is an exceptionally poor counseling technique.

We have all heard of examples of "interventions" for people with drug or alcohol abuse problems, when their friends and family get together and confront them with their problem. Pop culture sees this as a way to deal with this problem. Unfortunately, while this approach will usually get someone into counseling, it almost always dooms the counseling to failure. Hester and Miller (2003) found that confrontational counseling came in 45th place as a process for addressing alcohol abuse—so low on the list that the process can be expected to actually increase alcohol use.

Hidden commands are a way around this reactance or resistance. The command is hidden within a larger statement or question:

- I'm not going to tell you to <u>stop smoking now</u>.
- I don't know if <u>you are ready to change now</u>.
- How much better would you feel if you <u>start eating more appropriate portions at your meals</u>?

Assumptions

Another way to hide a directive is to simply assume that it is happening. The idea is to imply a change while focusing attention somewhere else.

- Before you start exercising, we should think about the best way to do it.
- When you quit smoking, I wonder how much better you will feel.
- I'm not sure what you would rather do first: Would you like to start some moderate exercise, or just eat more reasonable portions?
- Continue to relax now.
- Who will be the first to notice the changes you've made?
- What did you notice this week that was helpful for you?
- If everything was magically fixed while you were sleeping, what would you notice tomorrow which would let you notice change has happened?

Binds and The Illusion of Choice

A bind or illusion of choice offers the person a limited range of options. If the person emotionally buys into the illusion, they are "forced" to select from the choices, all of which are desirable from the point of view of the person who has offered the bind or illusion.

Of course, there are only an infinity of choices a person can make at any one moment, so the power of the illusion depends on the emotional connection—pacing or rapport—which has been established with the person.

Double binds create the possibility of an unconscious choice, which is currently hidden even from the client. Because the most powerful changes are created by the client, it can be helpful to introduce the possibility of a vague or unconscious choice which "will" happen. The setup of the bind still requires that the person will make a positive change.

Milton Erickson found that when he used double binds to help people create changes for themselves, the process worked wonderfully. However, if he tried to use double binds for selfish reasons—for his own gain and not the client's—the person would not know what was wrong, but would realize that something was desperately wrong. Typically the person would become angry (Erickson & Rossi, 1975).

Erickson also explored the emotional power of emotional binds—where one meaning was communicated nonverbally and emotionally while another was stated. An example of this would be the abusive parent or spouse who tells the victim "I love you." There is a bind or tension between the emotional context of the relationship (which is bad) and the verbal statement (which is good). This sort of bind is emotionally difficult for people to address. It is the basis of the cycle of abuse, where an abuser assaults the victim, then the two make up, then the abuse happens again, and the cycle repeats. We will look at simple verbal binds here, which can be very helpful to create positive change, but the hypnotist should be aware of emotional binds as well.

- Would you like to pay with cash, check or a credit card?
- Would you rather have dinner, go out for a drink, or just grab a cup of coffee?
- You don't know what day you are going to quit smoking. You don't know whether it will be the first of January, the middle of January, or the last part of January; but you are pretty sure it will happen before the 15th of February and you would give your soul to know the day.
- We both know that you are going to walk away from that destructive relationship. I don't know if you will do it today or later this week, but part of you already knows when it will be the best time for you to do it.

- Even though it seems it can't quite be this easy, there is an emotional part of you which is already thinking about change.
- You've probably only thought of a few ways to try to solve this problem, but your other-than-conscious can explore infinite possibilities.
- It does not matter how you make your hand go numb, or how your unconscious simply does it for you. The only thing that is important is that you know you can lose sensations as easily as flipping a switch.

Reflections

Motivational Interviewing (Miller and Rollnick, 2002) uses reflections as ways of facilitating client change. Sometimes the reflection simply exaggerates what the client said to get the client to take a step back:

- Client: My boss is always on my case! He never thinks I do anything right!

  Hypnotist: So it seems like there is no reason at all for him to be upset.

At other times reflections work off a client's emotional ambivalence. In Motivational Interviewing the idea is that a client is always ambivalent—part of the person wants change that another part does not. This tension provides a powerful emotional impetus for change. Notice the use of the word "and" rather than "but" in order to maintain the emotional tension:

- Client: I know you want me to talk to my boss about that, but I just can't do that!

  Hypnotist: On the one hand you're unhappy with what is happening at work, and on the other the idea of talking to your boss about it just seems impossible.

Shifting Focus

In Motivational Interviewing, instead of getting stuck on objections, the goal is to subtly ignore roadblocks thrown up by the client in order to help her or him imagine a solution.

- Client: I don't even want to be here. My mom made me come.

    Hypnotist: I can understand that. I'm sort of stuck here too—it's a beautiful day and I'd rather be outside. Since we are both stuck here, is there anything we could do that might be helpful for you?

Agreeing with a Twist

This Motivational Interviewing approach involves initially agreeing with a client objection, but shifting the meaning in the direction of a positive change. The key is to emphasize the client's personal choice and control.

- Client: You can't tell me how to run my life. You don't have to put up with the things I have to put up with. You have no idea what it is like!

    Hypnotist: You are absolutely right. This is your life, and I would never dream of telling you what to do. It seems like you have some decisions to make right now. I'd like to be your partner in this process, and I am wondering what you will decide to do.

Final Thoughts: Self-Efficacy

This last technique raises an important point, the idea of client control. This takes us to the important concept of psychological health. No matter what problem brings a client in the door, the goal is always to help that person become more healthy. One measure of psychological health is self-efficacy.

We all realize there are things that happen that are beyond our control. There are also things we do which are very much within our control. Self-efficacy is the belief that the things I do (my actions) have more to do with what my life is like; the out-of-my-control things are not as important. This contrasts with learned helplessness, the concept that things which are out of my control have more influence on my life than my own actions do. The key idea in self-efficacy is that my actions are meaningful, powerful, and significant in my life.

One persistent criticism of hypnosis, going back to the flamboyant days of Mesmer waving his hands and causing convulsions, is the idea that the hypnotist controls the subject. Clients often fear the possibility of losing control as part of the hypnosis process.

However, your unconscious is still you. All a hypnotist can do is engage the unconscious to create change. Erickson realized that the unconscious is a vast warehouse of positive resources that you can access to create a better life. In reality, your unconscious is much more than a passive storehouse. Emotion is the power of change. Your unconscious is a dynamic force always seeking your best. Even though it may be hemmed in or confused by destructive stories, the goal of the unconscious is always the health of the person. Hypnosis is a process to unleash the power of your unconscious to create positive change in your life. Your own positive unconscious will take you in the direction which is best for you.

APPENDIX: SOME ERICKSONIAN LANGUAGE PATTERNS

Hypnosis is the art of suggestion, and involves inviting the client to create his or her own solutions. Direct advice or confrontation is rarely helpful as a way to facilitate change. Framing suggestions in an inferred or indirect way can, on the other hand, be very helpful. The following are a number of phrases which can be used to couch suggestions and frame the conversation. Remember, the goal is not to tell the client what to do, but to invite him or her to create her or his own healing.

- I wonder if...
- Can you imagine what would happen if...
- What would it be like if...
- Can you imagine how it would be if...
- Suppose, for a moment...
- Just pretend...
- I won't tell you (to)...
- Maybe you'll dream of...
- People can, you know...
- You probably already know...
- You might try to think of...
- How would it feel if...
- One might just...
- I could tell you...but I won't.

- One might, you know...
- Sooner or later you'll want/resolve...
- You are able to...
- You might want to...
- You could...
- Eventually...
- A person might/could...
- You might not have noticed...
- You may find/get/want/like...
- One doesn't really have to...
- Can you really...
- Can you appreciate/allow/enjoy...
- You might notice...
- You don't have to...
- A person may...
- I don't know... I don't know if...
- You might want to...now...
- Would you like to see...
- Some people...(but you don't...)
- You might not know...
- Don't think that...
- ...but that's not important right now...
- How would it be if...
- Maybe you haven't...maybe you have...I don't know...

REFERENCES

Arons, H. (1961). *New master course in hypnotism.*
  Irvington, NJ: Power Publishers.
Baliki, M. H., Petre, B., Torbey, S., Herrmann, K. M.,
  Huang, L., Schnitzer, T. J., Fields, H. L., & Apkarian,
  A. V. (2012). Corticostriatal functional connectivity
  predicts transition to chronic back pain. *Nature
  Neuroscience*, advance online publication, 1-5.
Benedetti, F., Mayberg, H. S., Wager, t. D., Stohler, C. S., &
  Zubieta, J. (2005). Neurobiological mechanisms of
  the placebo effect. *The Journal of Neuroscience,
  25*(45), 10390 –10402.
Blakeslee, S. (2006, January 10). Cells that read minds.
  The New York Times. Retrieved from
  http://www.nytimes.com/2006/01/10/science/10m
  irr.html?pagewanted=all
Carlat, D. (2010, April 19). Mind over meds. *The New York
  Times.* Retrieved from
  http://www.nytimes.com/2010/04/25/magazine/2
  5Memoir-t.html
Coghlan, A. (2010, July 26). We humans can mind-meld
  too. *New Scientist, 2771.* Retrieved from
  http://www.newscientist.com/article/dn19220-we-
  humans-can-mindmeld-too.html
Cojan, Y., Waber, L., Schwartz, S. Rossier, L., Foster, A., &
  Vuilleumier, P. (2009). The brain under self-control:
  Modulation of inhibitory and monitoring cortical
  networks during hypnotic paralysis. *Neuron, 62,* 862-
  875.

Cojan, Y., Waber, L., Carruzzo, A., Vuilleumier, P. (2009). Motor inhibition in hysterical conversion paralysis. *NeuroImage, 47,* 1026–1037.

Crawford, H.J., Gur, R.C., Skolnick, B., Gur, R.E., & Benson, D.M. (1993). Effects of hypnosis on regional cerebral blood flow during ischemic pain with and without suggested hypnotic analgesia. *International Journal of Psychophysiology, 15,* 181-195.

de Shazer, S. (1997). Radical Acceptance. *Family Systems and Health, 15,* 375-378.

Ellenberger, H. F. (1970). *The Discovery of the unconscious: The history and evolution of dynamic psychiatry.* New York: Basic Books.

Erickson, M.H., & Rossi, E.L. (1975). Varieties of Double Bind. *The American Journal of Clinical Hypnosis, 17,* 143-157, in Erickson, M.H., & Rossi, E.L. (ed.). (1980). *The collected papers of Milton H. Erickson on hypnosis. Volume I: Nature of hypnosis and suggestion.* New York: Irvington Publishers, Inc., 412-420. Retrieved from http://www.scribd.com/doc/11320394/Erickson-Collected-Papers-Vol1

Faymonville, M.E., Laureys, S., Degueldre, C., Fiore, G.D., Luxen, A. Franck, G., Lamy, M., & Maquet, P. (2000). Neural Mechanisms of Antinociceptive Effects of Hypnosis. *Anesthesiology, 92,* 1257–1267. Retrieved from http://journals.lww.com/anesthesiology/toc/2000/05000

Feldman, J. B. (1985). The work of Milton Erickson: A multisystem model of eclectic therapy. *Psychotherapy, 22,* 154-162.

Forer, B. R. (1949) The Fallacy of Personal Validation: A classroom Demonstration of Gullibility, *Journal of Abnormal Psychology, 44,* 118-121.

Gruzelier, J., Gray, M. & Horn, P. (2002). The involvement of frontally modulated attention in hypnosis and hypnotic susceptibility: Cortical evoked potential evidence. *Contemporary Hypnosis, 19*(4), 179-189.

Hammond, D.C. (2007). Review of the efficacy of clinical hypnosis with headaches and migraines.

International Journal of Clinical and Experimental Hypnosis, 55(2), 207–219.

Hart, C. L., Ksir, C., & Ray, O. (2009). *Drugs, Society, and Human Behavior.* New York: McGraw-Hill.

Havens, R.A., & Walters, C. (1989). *Hypnotherapy scripts: A neo-Ericksonian approach to persuasive healing.* New York: Brunner/Mazel Publishers.

Hester, R.K. & Miller, W.R. (2003). *Handbook of alcoholism treatment approaches* (3rd ed). Boston: Allyn and Bacon.

Hogan, K. (2005). *The science of influence.* Hoboken: NJ: John Wiley & Sons, Inc.

Howard, G.S. (1989). *A tale of two stories: Excursions into a narrative approach to psychology.* Notre Dame, IN: Academic.

Insufficient sleep Is a public health epidemic. (2013, March 14). Centers for Disease Control and Prevention. Retrieved from: http://www.cdc.gov/features/dssleep/

Integration of Behavioral and Relaxation Approaches Into the Treatment of Chronic Pain and Insomnia. (1995, October 16-18). Technology Assessment Conference Statement (pp. 1-34). National Institutes of Health. Retrieved from: http://consensus.nih.gov/1995/1995BehaviorRelax PainInsomniata017html.htm

Jamieson, G.A., & Sheehan, P.W. (2004). An empirical test of Woody and Bowers's dissociated control theory of hypnosis. *The International Journal of Clinical and Experimental Hypnosis, 52*(3), 232-249.

Jennings, L., & Skovholt, T. M. (1999). The cognitive, emotional, and relational characteristics of master therapists. *Journal of Counseling Psychology, 46*(1), 3-11.

Johansen, J.W., & Sebel, P.S. (2000). Development and clinical application of electroencephalographic bispectrum monitoring, *Anesthesiology, 93*, 1336–1344.

Judson, O. (2010, May 4). Enhancing the placebo. *The New York Times.* Retrieved from

http://www.nytimes.com/2010/05/04/opinion/04j
udson.html

Kandel, E. R. (1998). A new intellectual framework for
Psychiatry. *American Journal of Psychiatry, 155*(4),
457-469.

Kirsch, I., & Lynn, S. J. (1995). The altered state of
hypnosis: Changes in the theoretical landscape.
American Psychologist, 50(10), 846-858.

Kirsch, I., Moore, T. J., Scoboria, A., & Nicholls, S. S.
(2002). The emperor's new drugs: An analysis of
antidepressant medication data submitted to the
U.S. Food and Drug Administration. *Prevention &
Treatment, 5*(1), No pagination specified.

Lilenfeld, S. O., & Arkowitz, H. (2009). Is hypnosis a
distinct form of consciousness? *Scientific American.*
Retrieved from
http://www.scientificamerican.com/article.cfm?id=is
-hypnosis-a-distinct-form

Meyer, N. (Director). (1982). *Star trek II: The wrath of Khan*
[Motion picture]. United States: Paramount Pictures.

Miller, W. (1998). *Toward a motivational definition and
understanding of addiction.* MI Nordic. Retrieved from
http://www.motiverandesamtal.org/miwiki/Toward
%20a%20Motivational%20Definition

Miller, W. R., & Rollnick, S. (2002). *Motivational
interviewing: Preparing people for change* (2nd ed.).
New York: The Guilford Press.

Montgomery, G. H., David, D., Winkel, D., Silverstein, J. H.,
& Bovbjerg, D. H. (2002). The effectiveness of
adjunctive hypnosis with surgical patients: A meta-
analysis. *Anesthesia & Analgesia, 94*, 1639-1645.

Ortigue, S., Bianchi-Demicheli, F., Patel, N., Frum, C., &
Lewis, J. W. (2010). Neuroimaging of love: fMRI
meta-analysis evidence toward new perspectives in
sexual medicine. *Journal of Sexual Medicine, 7*(11),
3541-3552.

Plassman, H., O'Doherty, J., Shiv, B., & Rangel, A. (2008).
Marketing actions can modulate neural
representations of experienced pleasantness.
Proceedings of the National Academy of Sciences, 105,
1050-1054.

Ray, O. (2004). How the mind hurts and heals the body. *American Psychologist, 59*(1), 29-40.

Rizzolatti, G. & Craighero, L. (2004). The mirror-neuron system. Annual Review of *Neuroscience, 27*, 169-192.

Rowling, J. K. (2007). *Harry Potter and the deathly hallows.* New York: Scholastic.

Sagan, S. (1996). *The demon-haunted world: Science as a candle in the dark.* New York: Random House.

Schjoedt, U., Stødkilde-Jørgensen, H., Geertz, A.W., Lund, T.E., & Roepstorff, A. (2009). The power of charisma – perceived charisma inhibits the frontal executive network of believers in intercessory prayer. *Social Cognitive and Effective Neuroscience, 4*, 199-207. Retrieved from http://scan.oxfordjournals.org/content/early/2010/03/12/scan.nsq023.full.pdf+html

Schulz-Stübner, S., Krings, T., Meister, I., Rex, S., Thron, A., & Rossaint, R. (2004). Clinical hypnosis modulates functional magnetic resonance imaging signal intensities and pain perception in a thermal stimulation paradigm. *Regional Anesthesia & Pain Medicine, 29*, 549-556.

Shor, R.E., & Orne, E.C. (1962). *Harvard group scale of hypnotic susceptibility, form A.* Harvard University. Retrieved from http://ist-socrates.berkeley.edu/~kihlstrm/PDFfiles/Hypnotizability/HGSHSAScript.pdf

Stephens, G.J., Silbert, L.J., & Hasson, U. (2010). Speaker–listener neural coupling underlies successful communication. *Proceedings of the National Academy of Sciences, 107*(32), 14425-14430 Retrieved from http://www.pnas.org/content/early/2010/07/13/1008662107.full.pdf+html

Steinbeck, J. (1954) *Sweet Thursday.* New York: Penguin.

Stossel, J. (2007). *Myths, lies and downright stupidity.* New York: Hyperion.

Syracuse University (2010, October 25). Falling in love only takes about a fifth of a second, research reveals. *ScienceDaily.* Retrieved from http://www.sciencedaily.com-/releases/2010/10/101022184957.htm

Thakkar, V. G. (2013, April 27). Diagnosing the wrong deficit. *The New York Times*. Retrieved from http://www.nytimes.com/2013/04/28/opinion/sunday/diagnosing-the-wrong-deficit.html?pagewanted=all&_r=0

Vergano, D. (2010, July 27). Mind meld: Brain cells synchronize during good conversations. *USA Today*. Retrieved from http://content.usatoday.com/communities/sciencefair/post/2010/07/mind-meld-neurons-conversation-brain/1

Weitzenhoffer, A.M., Hilgard, E.R., & Kihlstrom, J.F. (1962). *Stanford hypnotic susceptibility scale, form C.* Stanford University. Retrieved from http://socrates.berkeley.edu/~kihlstrm/PDFfiles/Hypnotizability/SHSSC%20Script.pdf

Zubieta, J, Smith, Y. R., Bueller, J. A., Xu, Y., Kilbourn, M. R., Jewett, D. M. Meyer, C. R., Koeppe, R. A., & Stohler, C. S. (2001). Regional mu opioid receptor regulation of sensory and affective dimensions of pain. *Science, 293*(5528), 311-315.

INDEX

ABOUT THE AUTHOR

Fredric Mau has practiced hypnosis professionally since 2004, and has had his own practice since 2006. He is a professional counselor and a National Guild of Hypnotists board-certified hypnotherapist and certified instructor of hypnosis. Mau is an accomplished public speaker. He holds a D.Min., a M.A. in professional counseling, and an M.Div. He lives near the burg of Irmo, South Carolina with his wife Sandy, his children and adoring dog, Buckley. If you would like to engage him as an instructor in hypnosis, for a speech or presentation, for therapy, or would like to provide feedback on this book, please contact him at WatermarkColumbia.com

Made in the USA
Lexington, KY
22 April 2016